THE REJUVENATION PROJECT

The Rejuvenation Project: To Live on Fire for Christ Without Burning Out

This book is set in the typeface *Athelas* designed by Veronika Burian and Jose Scaglione.

Hardcover ISBN: 978-1-955546-41-6
Paperback ISBN: 978-1-955546-56-0

A Publication of *Tall Pine Books*
119 E Center Street, Suite B4A | Warsaw, Indiana 46580
www.tallpinebooks.com

| 1 23 23 20 16 02 |

Published in the United States of America

THE REJUVENATION PROJECT

TO LIVE ON FIRE FOR CHRIST WITHOUT BURNING OUT

CALEB STAYTON

I'D LIKE TO HONOR:

My wife and love, Rachel.
My girls, Cora and Joanna.
My parents and role models, Fred and Cheryl.
My friend, mentor, and editor, Erin Loechner.
My Church, Sonrise Church.

CONTENTS

Introduction: The Rejuvenated Way 1

1. God is Good 7
2. God is Big 19
3. Washed by the Word 31
4. The God Company 49
5. Presence 61
6. Obedience 77
7. Forgiveness 93
8. Purpose 111
9. Character 127
10. The Spark to Burnout 137
11. The Heavenly Pace 149
12. The Gardener Prunes and Grafts 165
13. Shut Up and Pray 179
14. We Can't Outgive God 189
15. Be Fruitful and Multiply 203
16. The Power of Why 217

Final Thoughts: 225
About the Author 227
Endnotes 228

INTRODUCTION

THE REJUVENATED WAY

AS CHRISTIANS, WE serve a God who is the source of all love, hope, joy, peace, goodness, righteousness, compassion, and life; and yet, Christians are continually expressing how tired, worn out, burnt out, emotionally spent, apathetic, uncreative, and ticked off we are. What's up with that? If God lives in us, why do those two lists look so different? In our western Christian society, we celebrate the new up-and-coming leaders while we hear about the sinful, secret lives of those we promoted just decades earlier. Shouldn't our lives grow stronger the longer we walk with Christ? This doesn't seem to be the norm.

What happened to all the high school commitments to Christ that claimed "I will do whatever you want me to do and go wherever you want me to go, God."? Why are words like "cranky," "mean," and "out of touch" used to describe older generations? Why do so few people finish life strongly in love with God? I believe every Christian desires to hear the words from Jesus' mouth "Well done, good and faithful servant!" I know I do! But how can we be so sure that we are going to hear that from Him if our spiritual lives are in slow decline for years and decades leading up to that fateful day?

When were *you* the most faithfully following God? I pray it is today. If not, I pray it starts trending in a new direction.

I am a follower of Jesus. I seek to replicate His ways in my life and live my life using everything God has made available to us. I understand Jesus is no new name to you. He is the Alpha and the Omega, the Lord Almighty, The Great Shepherd, The Prince of Peace, The Lion of Judah. He is Wisdom and Glory and Honor and Power and Majesty and Everlasting Life. His love has no end. Death couldn't conquer Him. Every knee will bow to Him. We are talking about the Messiah, The Savior of the World, Jesus Christ.

If you really take a step back to ponder, having a life that looks just like Jesus, the person that possesses everything great, is a pipe dream. Trying to follow and replicate my life to look like someone who possesses all of these great names seems unattainable. How could anybody even dare to live a life that looks like Jesus? Well, the answer to that is simply another great quality of His: *grace*. In all of God's greatness and majesty, He has made a way for us to follow Him and be with Him. We do not seek to be like Jesus on our own power, but through His power we are able to become like Him. Jesus is the journey and the destination all packed into one. We do not seek to be like Jesus for our own glory, but rather in preparation for the day we *will* be one with Him. You will meet Jesus someday. He will come back to this earth. It is not open to interpretation. When He returns, what will He find? Or, perhaps more importantly: *Whom* will He find?

I certainly desire to be found faithful at the end of my life. God willing, I still have many years to walk with him. This book isn't written on the back of my personal experiences, but rather on the wisdom of those who have walked faithfully before me. Thankfully, I have had faithful generations before me that have finished this life genuinely in love with God. I am writing to connect the faithful generations before me with the faithful ones to come after me. I am also writing this book because I recognize there will likely be a day that I need it for my own life. Nobody is immune to troubles. In fact, it is one thing Jesus promises us (John 16:33). Rather than pretend I am the exception to Jesus' promise, I want to embrace this reality and develop a game plan to follow when my world feels like it is crashing in. This book is for me. The guy who wrote The Rejuvenation Project needs it the most.

Rather than just embrace the plan myself, I want to share the contents with you because I realize no one is immune to burnout. We want to live on fire for Christ without burning out. When I speak of "fire," I am talking about our passion for God and His purposes for our life. The true flame of God is unique like no other. As we see with the burning bush, it burns without burning up (Exodus 3:2). If we live by our own passions and purposes, we will be like a natural fire. It consumes whatever it possesses.

Maybe you have served God faithfully for years and now feel like you have no more fuel for the fire. Maybe your life was going fine until a storm came and snuffed you out and you wonder if you will ever recover again. Maybe you have been trying to get the fire started in your life, but it just seems like no flame can take hold for long. Regardless of how you got here, you wonder how you could ever recover a pile of smoldering ash. The beauty is, it's not up to you.

The truth is, we already have the answer to faith that burns out. His name is Jesus. Rekindle your love for Him again. Go back to your first love. Your love shouldn't grow dim as you age. The flame should grow stronger and burn brighter. After all, we are called to be the light of the world (Matthew 5:14). It's hard to be a light when you are burnt out. None of us knows when God will take us home or when He will show up, but we should ensure that we are at our best when He does.

That is the premise of this book. The contents here are a roadmap to make your last days on earth your best days in Christ. To live a life on fire for Christ without burning out. My prayer for you as you read this book is that your heart would be stirred to seek after Jesus. As you read the pages that follow, I do not want you to read to get a checklist. I want these words to bring you into the love and intimacy that Christ gives each of us. I want the characteristics of your life and the characteristics of your God to align. I want your heart to be filled with passion. To make your heart and your mind communicate again. To feel. To hunger. To learn.

God doesn't reveal everything to us on our 16th birthday. God teaches over time. The longer we faithfully walk with God, the more we know Him. The problem is, we have had decades of leaders burnout before they ever reach their golden years. The consequences are great because we have thousands of books and sermons written from the wisdom of a 30-year-old, but very few written from the 85-year-old. No offense to myself, but the book I write when I am 72 years old will be better than when I am 27 years old. The contribution I want The Rejuvenation Project to bring to the Church will be the future wisdom that God reveals to those who walk faithfully with Him into their old age.

The Rejuvenation Project was conceived shortly after I was born. My father was sitting in his office at the local church he was pastoring. He had just finished listening to a cassette tape about finding your mission in life. He scribbled on a piece of paper a mission statement he thought up on the spot. Though it seemed spontaneously written on the paper, the mission had always been written on his heart: *To live a Kingdom life that produces other Kingdom leaders and families.* In fact, it appears this mission was also written on my heart. My dad has lived a Kingdom life and passed it on to me. Now I get to write to you about it and expand it. My dad and I launched The Rejuvenation Project together in 2020 as a way to encourage people to live on fire for God in the life He has planned for them.

Rejuvenate means "to make young or youthful again: give new vigor to."[1] I want every reader to be rejuvenated in their relationship with God. I use the word "Project" not because I believe you are a project, but because I believe we all need to work together to take the rejuvenating power of Jesus Christ to the world and I want you to get involved in the project Jesus asked us to carry out when He left this earth. This book doesn't have to be read in one sitting. It is very likely that you read a chapter and then have to spend days, weeks, or months putting it into practice. Please read thoroughly. If you skim and move fast through it, you won't see the results you are desiring. You can't fake rejuvenation. Rejuvenation must be lived, not read. I believe these lessons are wisdom from God, but remember they are written by a human. Test them against the scriptures yourself and don't treat them as the be-all and end-all. My words are just a starting place to send you on your own journey with Christ. Read a chapter and then pursue your King. Come back and read another, then go experience more of His love. I hope this book will be a guide you frequent often to stir up passions in your heart for God.

At the end of every chapter there will be a "Rejuvenation Project" for you. These are assignments to help you take the material and begin to apply it to your life. May each of these prompts be a helpful starting place for you in your own Rejuvenation journey. Let me pray for you as we begin:

> *God, I pray for the individual reading this book. I know it is by no accident they are reading this. Even before they start reading, Holy Spirit, would you pour over them with your love wherever they are? If they are burnt out and hurt, I pray you spark alive in them now. If they are in a healthy place, I pray for increased passion, health, and blessings. Please help their heart and eyes to be open to what you want to reveal to them. Take my words and make them yours, God, for the glory of your name. Amen*

CHAPTER ONE

GOD IS GOOD

I CAN HEAR it now. It's Sunday morning. The liturgist stands up in church and exclaims, "God is good!" "All the time!" the congregation replies as they wipe the sleep from their eyes. "All the time!" She exhorts. They instinctively respond, "God is good." It's a familiar script you may remember if you grew up in church, especially if you are a pastor's kid like I am. All religious clichés aside, "God is good." may be the most important foundational belief necessary for finishing life strongly in love with God.

God's goodness may be one of the most obvious, and yet, oddly mystifying concepts to explore. Of course, we all say God is good because why would we serve a *bad* God? However, the more we examine the world we live in, the more complicated it seems. Where is God's goodness in the injustices of the world? Where is God's goodness in a young girl sold into sex trade? Where is God's goodness when a father dies in a car accident leaving behind a pregnant wife and two young kids? Where is the good in terminal illness? In abusive parents? How do we paint a picture of God's goodness on the canvas of our merciless world? Honestly, the more we try, the harder it gets. I could spend the rest of this book listing all the bad things in this world, but essentially it leads us all to questions like, "Why do bad things happen to good people?" and "Why doesn't God help me?"

Many have sought to understand why the world is the way it is. Oftentimes, the more one searches for answers, the more questions they have. This process repeats itself until one is too lost to know where they even started the train of thought. God is good. A statement so simple, yet our minds often can't begin to comprehend the goodness of God in the midst of our world and struggles. My suggestion? Stop trying!

Is it good to seek out answers to questions? Absolutely. Proverbs 25:2 says, "It is the glory of God to conceal a matter; to search out a matter is the glory of kings" (NIV). Jeremiah 29:13 says, "You will seek me and find me when you seek me with all your heart" (NIV). And Jesus himself intentionally spoke in parables so that we would have to seek Him. It's clear in scripture that we should seek God and His ways. However, there is one area that we don't - and shouldn't - need to seek very long for: *to decide God is good.*

Beliefs are simply choices we make based on information. The source for most of that information is our own life experiences. Using our life experience to form decisions usually works out well for us, but there is one area in which it doesn't: deciding whether or not God is good.

If I asked you if you believe God is good, you might quickly respond, "Of course!" However, we won't really know the answer to this question until the storms of life come. Is God still good even when things aren't going well? Contemplating God's goodness in the midst of tragedy can lead some to walk away from faith altogether or, at minimum, halt their faith for many years.

In 2020, everyone faced a trial of a worldwide pandemic. What I noticed through the years navigating a pandemic was that some Christians grew stronger in their faith, whereas others grew much more distant. Why is that? If a storm hits us all, shouldn't we all be affected the same way? If the circumstances we face determine what happens to us, then we should all have ended up in the same place, right? But quite the opposite happened. We became more divided. We all faced the same storm, but each person was impacted differently.

If life is beating you up, circumstances aren't the main problem. The belief system is the main problem. That's why some people go through trials and tragedies and come out stronger on the other side, while others don't. Jesus preaches it like this:

> Therefore, everyone who hears these words of mine and puts them into practice is like a wise man who built his house on the rock. The rain came down, the streams rose, and the winds blew and beat against that house; yet it did not fall, because it had its foundation on the rock. But everyone who hears these words of mine and does not put them into practice is like a foolish man who built his house on sand. The rain came down, the streams rose, and the winds blew and beat against that house, and it fell with a great crash. (Matthew 7:24-27, NIV)

The problem is not the storm. The problem is the house, specifically the foundation. The storm descends on all people, the righteous and the wicked. It doesn't discriminate. Rather than try to stop a storm, let's instead focus our efforts on building a foundation that will survive the next storm in our life. No storm can wipe us out if we have a stronger foundation.

What's the foundation, then, that we build on? Well, according to the passage, Jesus says it's hearing the word of God *and* putting it into practice. Jesus uses this specific parable to finish up the most significant sermon of His life; a sermon that modern preachers would need at *least* a 10-week sermon series to preach. Jesus uses the parable to emphasize to His listeners the importance of not just hearing His words, but applying them to their lives. If we are being real with ourselves, the "putting it into practice" part is probably the difference needed in all our lives. The way to build a strong foundation is to hear *and* to apply. To help us better understand the application of the sermon, let's check out the beginning.

> Blessed are the poor in spirit, for theirs is the kingdom of heaven. Blessed are those who mourn, for they will be comforted. Blessed are the meek, for they will inherit the earth. (Matthew 5:3-5, NIV)

This passage continues in this pattern and is chock-full of theology, most of which is beyond my intellect right now. I can tell you one thing that sticks out to me though... It's counterintuitive. I am used to associating blessing with overflow, yet the first few verses start out with Jesus calling those who are poor in spirit, mourning, and meek the ones who are blessed. Those aren't the adjectives I would use to describe a blessed person. That's precisely what we have to understand: our ways are not His ways. Our thoughts are not His thoughts. My eyes cannot see what His eyes see. What we think about God doesn't actually change God, it changes *us*. Many of us are looking at our circumstances and putting God on trial for them because they don't follow our logic. God has a different scorecard than our human nature does.

We cannot start the process of rejuvenation on a broken foundation. We have to build on the rock. To build on the rock, we cannot build on our experiences and opinions. Proverbs 14:22, says, "There is a way that appears to be right, but in the end it leads to death" (NIV). Scripture screams at us, "Don't be deceived!" Rather than using our experiences and intellect to mold our faith, we must begin to let our faith mold our experiences. This shift will bring about a rejuvenated life.

My dad and I will occasionally dabble in woodworking projects. While we work on our projects, we live by the motto "A good carpenter and a bad carpenter both make mistakes. A good one just knows how to hide them." It's how we make ourselves feel better for making mistakes while we work. A common mistake that I make is in my measuring. My measurements are close, but sometimes my cuts are a little off the mark and it throws off the whole project. I am not far off, but off nonetheless. When we are building something, we cannot afford to just be close. We have to be spot on.

To bring this into a spiritual perspective, I am afraid that many of us are okay with believing God is 95% good. None of us want to build our homes just 95% well, so we mustn't settle for that percentage in our spiritual foundations either. If we are only 95% certain that God is good, our future is burnout and we won't live our last day as our best. We may survive a lot of storms, but we won't survive the big one. The storm is coming and we need to have a foundation that is 100% ready to withstand it. Any niggling doubt of God's goodness will torment us with every growing gale.

God wants us to seek after the questions of our lives, but we must seek those questions only within the belief that God is good. We must peer from that standpoint alone, from the absolute principal foundation that God is good. From that vantage point, we are more apt to gain perspective for our life. It takes a step of faith to choose to believe God is good. This sounds foolish to start with a "blind" belief, but it's only foolish if we have a different scorecard. Remember: we are playing God's game. Faith is a priority to God.[2]

BACK TO THE BEGINNING

When God made the universe and all of creation, He described it with one adjective. If we read Genesis 1, we will notice after most of the days of creation, God says, "It was good." Creation reflects the creator. We create from who we are. Take biology for example, my offspring are humans because I am human. Dogs create dogs. Birds create birds. Fish create fish. You get the point. God can only make a good creation if He is.

If we continue in creation we will discover that we are made in the image of God. That means that God made *you* good. This isn't too hard to grasp for us; many people have a bias that they are good. But many people also don't believe they are good. Regardless of where you camp out, God made you good. We were made in His likeness, which is so many things, but we shouldn't overlook the first words he used to describe us. "God saw all that he had made, and it was *very* good" (Genesis 1:31, NIV). The creator instills what

His creation is and then creation reflects it back to Him. It's a never-ending flow of goodness between God and humanity.

If you are still struggling with the idea of God's goodness, then you probably struggle with your own goodness. You may say, "Of course, I am the worst of sinners. There is nothing good in me." Fair, but it was not always this way. God first made human beings good before we ever became evil.

Out of all creation, one of the most fascinating things God made was in the center of the Garden of Eden. "In the middle of the garden were the tree of life and the tree of the knowledge of good and evil" (Genesis 2:9b, NIV). "And the Lord God commanded the man, 'You are free to eat from any tree in the garden; but you must not eat from the tree of the knowledge of good and evil, for when you eat from it you will certainly die'" (Genesis 2:16-7, NIV). This is significant and says so much about our God and creator. In the midst of this good creation, He created choice. God exists in relationship and His deepest desire seems to be relationship with us. In order for there to be a relationship, there has to be love. In order for there to be love, there has to be choice. We are not forced to love God; we *choose* to love God. When God placed those trees in the garden, He presented his intent for creation. He gave us choices because He wants to be intimately in love with us.

Unfortunately, the story doesn't jump straight to a happy ending. Adam and Eve disobeyed God and ate the fruit of the tree by their choice, ushering in the evil, sin, and toil we know today. The great news is, God still has a plan. His name is Jesus Christ. Jesus came to the earth to die for our sins. Romans 5:6-8 says, "You see, at just the right time, when we were still powerless, Christ died for the ungodly. Very rarely will anyone die for a righteous person, though for a good person someone might possibly dare to die. But God demonstrates his own love for us in this: While we were still sinners, Christ died for us" (NIV). There is that word "good" again. Someone may die for a righteous person, but Christ died for all of us *sinners*. Why? Because He was redeeming our goodness. Jesus takes us back to the goodness of the garden. If we were never good in the first place, why would we need to be redeemed?

Ultimately, the gospel story is a story of redeeming goodness.

2 Peter 1:3-8 says:

> His divine power has given us everything we need for a godly life through our knowledge of him who called us by his own glory and *goodness*. Through these he has given us his very great and precious promises, so that through them you may participate in the divine nature, having escaped the corruption in the world caused by evil desires. For this very reason, make every effort to add to your faith *goodness*; and to goodness, knowledge; and to knowledge, self-control; and to self-control, perseverance; and to perseverance, godliness; and to godliness, mutual affection; and to mutual affection, love. For if you possess these qualities in increasing measure, they will keep you from being ineffective and unproductive in your knowledge of our Lord Jesus Christ. (NIV)

There are two main things to contemplate from this passage. First, God's glory and goodness is the catalyst for our calling and a godly life. Many people desire to know the answer to the question, "What's my purpose in life?" We will get into our purpose in life more in later chapters, but before we answer that question, we have to first ask ourselves, "Do I believe God is good?"

Let's think about cell phones. If we want to talk on the phone with someone, we each need a phone connected to the network. We cannot call someone that doesn't have a phone. Let's take that idea into this passage. God wants to call us. He does so by His glory and goodness. If God is going to call us through His glory and goodness, then those two attributes will be the conduit we need in place to hear God's call on our lives. Any inkling that God isn't good sabotages our purpose in Christ.

Second, Peter describes a progression for keeping us effective and productive in our knowledge of God. That alone should perk our ears since we are seeking to live a rejuvenated life. The fact of the matter is that goodness sets the foundation for everything else. Love is not the first step; love is the pinnacle. The first step is *goodness*. Let's use the building analogy. Peter is describing a structure of what true faith in God is. So, think about your "faith" as the entire house. Your faith is made up of different parts like a house. The first thing Peter says to add to our faith house is goodness.

It doesn't take too much knowledge to understand that any building starts from the ground up. Peter lays the foundation of faith as goodness. From there we add to our faith knowledge, self-control, perseverance, godliness, mutual affection and then love. Peter also suggests that we are to possess these qualities in increasing measure. So ultimately, we have to have the greatest measure of love, but we will never get to that part if we do not start the faith foundation on goodness. Not our goodness though. The foundation of goodness is Jesus Christ and it is He that makes us good.

My brother-in-law runs a car detailing business. He tells me that some people will clean their cars before having them professionally detailed because they are ashamed at how dirty their car is. That's dumb all around. Why clean a car before you pay to have someone else clean it? The reason is the same whether it's cleaning our cars or our hearts: it's shame. We feel shame that we are so messy, and we feel like we need to clean it up to present ourselves to God. But no matter how much pre-cleaning we do, we are still filthy.

I once was sharing the gospel with a man at a wedding and I finally came to the question, "Would you surrender your life to Jesus tonight?" He agreed that Jesus was probably the best decision for his life, but he assured me that he had done some things he wasn't proud of in the past and he needed to take care of those things before he could be good enough for Jesus. Despite my trying to persist that was unnecessary, he concluded he must clean up his life before giving it to Jesus. Later on down the road, he did end up praying a prayer of salvation, but many never feel "clean enough" to get to that point. If you are dirty, no amount of effort will ever make you clean. John the Baptist has a powerful statement when he sees Jesus, "Behold, the Lamb of God, who takes away the sin of the world!" (John 1:29, ESV). It's Jesus' job to clean us, but we must allow Him to do so.

Eric Gilmour says, "The command is to behold, not behave." The scripture says, "Behold, the Lamb of God who takes away the sin of the world." We think the scripture says, "Behave, the Lamb of God who takes away the sin of the world." We may have prayed a prayer of salvation, but deep down we are trying to make up for our shortcomings rather than just fixing our eyes on the Lamb of God who washes us white as snow.

Can I share a great truth? All we have to do is turn our eyes to Jesus. If we surrender our life and repent of our sins, we will be clean. I know we feel guilt for our past, but there is nothing we can do to clean it up. Heck, our world is messed up, and there is nothing we can do to make it clean either. God is not the problem. He is the solution. He is making all things new! He is redeeming His creation to its original goodness.

FINAL THOUGHTS ON GOODNESS

Let's address one more thing since we are talking about goodness. Have you ever had a situation in your life that originally you thought was bad, but ended up good? I can think of times in my life where an injury, a loss, a failure, or a disappointment actually lead me to a better future. I didn't always see it at the time, but hindsight proved the disappointments were actually launching pads for my future blessings. This begs the question, "Is God the one that caused the pain to begin with?" I dare not make a broad proclamation on behalf of God, but I do know that God works for the good of those who love him (Romans 8:28). As King David proclaims, "You have turned my mourning into joyful dancing" (Psalm 30:11, NLT).

God has a track record of turning pain into a greater purpose. If it were up to me, there are probably countless blessings that would have been missed simply because I would have written them off as suffering. Many of us make conclusions about good and bad based on our nearsighted view of human existence. God makes His determination of good based on his view of both ends of eternity. I want to trust His judgment for what is good for me. Thankfully, God reigns supreme and guides our paths despite our momentary conclusions. He turns our tears into victory! Aren't we glad?

Job chapter 38-42 is a section of scripture that helps bring my thinking into proper alignment with God's supreme nature and knowledge of our world. When I question what is going wrong in my life or around me, I answer with Job. Job had probably the worst fortune a man can have. In a short amount of time, most of his family died, his enemies took his possessions, his body became diseased, and his friends were far from supportive. For 37 chapters, Job and his pals are debating the ways of God and the world. Finally, God chimes in.

> Where were you when I laid the earth's foundation? Tell me, if you understand. Who marked off its dimensions? Surely you know! Who stretched a measuring line across it? On what were its footings set, or who laid its cornerstone—while the morning stars sang together and all the angels shouted for joy? (Job 38:4-7, NIV)

God continues to speak in this way for the next few chapters. Job is speechless. Halfway through God's questioning, Job puts his hand over his mouth and exclaims "I am unworthy—how can I reply to you?" (Job 40:4, NIV). God continues on His monologue of power and majesty until the end of the book. Here is Job's final reply: "Surely, I spoke of things I did not understand, things too wonderful for me to know. "You said, 'Listen now, and I will speak; I will question you, and you shall answer me.' My ears had heard of you but now my eyes have seen you. Therefore I despise myself and repent in dust and ashes" (Job 42:3-6, NIV).

Job had to repent of speaking like he knew what was going on because God is just too big for us to know His ways completely. We too should be a little slower to jump to conclusions about what is good or what God is doing. His ways are higher than ours. We don't define what is good, and God is not subjected to our limitations.

When I was a young boy, I remember a time where my sister and I got into a disagreement. I can't remember exactly what about, but I do remember getting sent to my room to ponder what I had done and let my anger cool off. As I was sitting there, I knew that there was *no way* this conflict was my fault. I reasoned that this was all my sister's fault. I then realized that it couldn't be my sister's fault because she was born to my parents. So, it was my *parent's* fault for even giving birth to her! I then began to work up the family tree until I decided that all my troubles were Eve's fault. "Why on earth did she eat the fruit?" I reasoned. I finished my terrible fault-finding discourse through human history and reached my ultimate conclusion: everything must be God's fault.

This is a pretty incredible conclusion for a young boy no more than 8 years old. I remember distinctly believing at that moment that all my problems were because of God. If it all started from God, then all trouble gets traced back to Him, right? Many believe this same logic. It's a lie that Satan tried to plant in my life early because he knew it would cause a shaky house of faith to be built. If God is our problem, He cannot also be the solution. It's a flawed theology.

How ashamed I am that I ever had that idea! The whole internal dialogue was a mistake. It was my fault to begin with. I now know that I am the problem, and Jesus Christ is my solution.

Friends, I am tired of seeing people dead in their lives and blown over by storms they couldn't stand up in. We are never going to make it through the storms standing alone on our own. We have to build a house. Not only that, we have to build it on a foundation that can't be moved. We must build it on the foundation that God is good. Blueprints of a foundation won't save us either. We actually have to build it. We must put the words of Christ to practice. No matter what happens to us or others, He is good. He doesn't change when our life changes. He is always good. It may not make sense for what is going on in our life, but He is still good.

We do not need to have good things happen to us to decide that God is good.

Beliefs are just choices. Rather than letting a fallen world tell us who God is, take it from the source that He is good. This belief is the foundation. If God isn't good, then we can't be made good, then there is no need for the redeeming blood of Jesus. However, we were made good. By our choices, we left God's goodness. Thankfully, God made a way to bring us back to the original design through Jesus. I know I can't answer your deepest questions right now, but I can tell you where to start. Start by building a house made to weather any storm. Build it here, on God's unfathomable goodness.

THE REJUVENATION PROJECT

What is keeping you from believing God is good? Wrestle with it. Be honest with yourself. Maybe you have had some really bad things happen to you. Replay your situation from a new perspective. Don't view God as the instigator of your pain, but rather the solution. It shouldn't take you more than a few days to process and make a decision that God is good. Seriously! It shouldn't take long. You're not answering all your life questions, you are deciding the basis for which you will go about searching for the answers. It's a choice. It's simple. We cannot move on to a rejuvenated life if you don't believe God is completely good. We don't want to rebuild the house just for it to get blown over by another storm. If we are going to build, we are going to build this house right. We build on the foundation that God is good.

The prayer goes like this:

> *"God, you are good. I believe you made me good out of your own goodness and have redeemed me. From this day forward, I choose to build my house on the foundation that you are always good. I don't care what situation arises; my mind won't change. Jesus, thank you for dying on the cross to make me good again. I give you my life and I commit to your goodness. Amen."*

CHAPTER TWO

GOD IS BIG

GOD IS BIGGER than this plan. He is bigger than any system. He is outside of all definitions. The first step to recognizing the plan of God for our life is to realize nobody but God has that plan. I certainly do not have the plan for your life. I do have some tips that are helpful for living life on fire for Christ, but even then, I have run into roadblocks with each plan I make. For whatever reason, my plans don't always go to plan. Anybody else have an "Amen" for that?

Burnout doesn't just come because of sin or a lack of love for the Lord. Burnout ignites whenever we start following human plans more than God's plans for our life. Many times, human wisdom and godly wisdom will align seamlessly, but there will be other times they don't. Human plans have a tendency to be too rigid, and do not have the capacity to keep up with the movements of the Spirit. However, we shouldn't throw out structure and plans altogether because without structure, there is little room for God to do His sanctifying work in our lives. We must have plans and structures in our lives, but we must allow for flexibility within those plans to allow for God's natural movements. Even as we embark on the Rejuvenation Project, I urge each reader to hold this plan with a level of flexibility.

God's not dead; He is alive and active. A key characteristic for something that is alive is that it is moving or growing. We forget this aspect of God. Oftentimes, we see Jesus as a pearly gate, rather than a moving person. Our goal is to get through those pearly gates, rather than sit at the feet of our Lord, wherever He is at the time. We have a tendency to get an idea of who God is and what it means to follow Him and we fixate on this idea. We set these ideas as our ultimate goal of following Christ. We say things like: "Christians spend time with the Lord each day," "The most important thing is to share the gospel,"or "It's all about loving God and loving others." A very dangerous place any person can find themselves in is making an audacious claim that everything about God boils down to one item. God has no start and no end, so when we make claims that say, "It's all about_____," we are making efforts to comprehend God, but how could we completely comprehend the reality that God has no beginning and He is the ultimate of everything? He is the most creative. The ultimate judge. The most passionate lover. We don't realize our misalignment because God is so big that generally our nearsighted conclusions ring true, but in reality, they are just a fraction of who God is. This mistake is an innocent step that leads to our demise.

As humans, we can see life from a start and an end point. We have the point of conception and we can see the last breath. Two very specific moments. But God isn't this way. When we fixate on one thing, we miss everything else that God is. It would be like zooming in on a picture on our phone. Yes, what we are looking at is truly a part of the picture, but when we zoom in, we miss the bigger picture. This is what happens when we say, "The most important thing about following God is..." We zoom in so far that we unintentionally crop the rest of the nature of God out of our lives. This is a major deception of the enemy. We believe we have to go deeper to know God, but we actually need to go *bigger*. The truth of the matter is that more people are deceived by the things they are most certain of than the things they are uncertain of because our certainties constrict our perspective of God.

Proverbs 9:10 says, "The fear of the Lord is the beginning of wisdom" (NIV). Now, I have yet to hear of a person that didn't want wisdom in their life, but I have seen a lot of lifestyles that contradict that desire. Regardless, the first step to wisdom is the fear of the Lord. And I would like to suggest that the first step to fearing the Lord is realizing that He is bigger than us. It's a control issue. We have a false sense of security when we feel in control of our lives. When we acknowledge a power far greater than ours, it tramples our sense of power. Fear is not always a negative word. Fear in general increases our sense of awareness. If we are walking on a cliff 1,000 feet up, our fear helps us focus on each step we take so that we don't fall. Similarly, recognizing there is a God much bigger than us and one we cannot explain completely creates a sense of fear that initiates a recognition of Him with every step we take.

If I thought about God before every action, I am sure my life would reflect a life of wisdom. If our view of God feels perfectly clear and defined, it may be because we overestimate how powerful we are and don't realize how big and powerful He is. We think wisdom is being able to generate simple explanations that make sense to our minds, but wisdom comes when we live in the reality that God is big and He is moving and He doesn't fit into a human system. Do not underestimate this God we serve.

My dad likes to say, "For every mile of road, there are two miles of ditches." There are twice as many opportunities to go off the road than there are to stay on it. We get into the ditches of religion when we make absolute conclusions about the nature of God based on the zoomed in picture God is currently revealing to us. What characteristic of God are you most certain of? Likely, the answer to that question will identify the ditch you live in.

Have you ever been stuck on a decision? Should I work at job A or job B? Should I buy house A or house B? The best way to bring clarity to any decision we feel stuck on is to open up our search. If we are stuck between choosing between two things, we want to open up our search to choose between four to five choices. If somebody comes to me for advice when they feel stuck on an issue in life, the way I coach them to a real decision is to actually begin to give them more choices. If somebody is choosing between jobs, I'll ask, "Why are you working in the first place?" If you are choosing which house to buy, I'll say, "Why don't you rent instead?" The more outlandish my idea can be at that moment, the better. Why? Because it opens up the mind to more possibilities. If you feel stuck in faith, it may be because you have zoomed in too much. Zoom out and see that our God is bigger than anything. If our once vibrant faith has become stale, it's likely because we became fixated on one aspect of God and have missed the rest of His revelation to us.

I refer to Christians that get fixated on one aspect of faith as the "The Hokey Pokey Christian." You may know the song.

> You put your right foot in.
> You put your right foot out.
> You put your right foot in.
> And you shake it all about.
> You do the Hokey Pokey and you turn yourself around.
> *That's what it's all about!*

A trap that causes us to fall in and out of passion for Christ is actually the thing we believe "it's all about." This is where the faith roller coaster comes into effect. Up and down. In and out. I know life will naturally give us some ups and downs, but our passion for the Lord shouldn't follow the same pattern. We mustn't let our faith be stunted. We should do our best to never say again, "That's what it's all about."

Here is how this plays out in real life. For seasons of our life, God teaches us about a certain aspect of His nature. Let's say God is showing us true grace. This lesson is meaningful to all, but especially to us in that particular season. It changes our life so much that we begin to tell people, "Grace changed my life!" We continue to be radically moved by God's grace and we begin to say to others, "It all boils down to God's grace." This goes well for a period of time, because God's grace abounds and it really is amazing (Romans 5:20). However, 3-5 years down the road, we are no longer as moved by God's grace. We have become complacent. We are continuing the same patterns of sins we had when we first believed, and now we are numb to the "Sinner's Prayer." We lack the discipline an established Christian should have. We become embarrassed to approach the throne of grace for the 600th time, and are no longer sure if God still loves us or worse yet, if He is even real.

So what happened? In our appreciation of God's grace, we made it the central focus of our faith. With pure motives, we limited God. God showed us grace to start, but then He kept walking to show us more of His beauty, works, and nature, and we failed to follow because we fixated on the first thing He revealed to us. We must remember the lessons God teaches us over our lives, but we cannot park on just one thought. God has more to show us because He is bigger. God will emphasize some of His nature for a season so we can realize the great magnitude of His love, affection, grace, mercy, holiness, etc. By the end of our life, we will have enough seasons of God showing us different parts of Himself that we will truly begin to have a pure view of who God is and how He relates to His people.

Think about it like a sky-scrapper. The whole structure is the grandeur of God, and as He walks us through the structure, He points out what He is made out of. No one thing is the most important building material. If we fixate on one thing, we wouldn't necessarily be wrong because it is a part of the structure, but we just miss the beauty of the bigger picture. As God desires to mold us to look like Jesus, He builds. One thing at a time. Not all at once. Yes, God's grace is a major part of the building, but there is more because He is bigger!

I have a sweet friend that has helped me so much in following God. I remember a season where I prayed for people and they kept being physically healed. I was astonished at God's power and also became more prideful by the day because I felt I had certainly cracked the code of God. I remember all of a sudden nobody was being healed anymore when I prayed. I was talking to my friend trying to figure out how I had offended God or where I was sinning and he simply said, "If you kept seeing people get healed, would you ever learn more about God?" He nailed it. God wasn't taking a gift away from me or punishing me. He was desiring to show me more things. He didn't want me to become the guy that healed everybody, He wanted me to be His son.

God's desire isn't to make us do things for Him. He is perfectly capable of handling His own work. His desire is for us to know Him. It would kill us if He revealed everything about Himself to us in one moment. In His mercy and patience, He chooses to pour Himself out to us slowly over time and maybe in a different order for each person. We have to be able to adapt to where He is and how He wants to pour Himself out to us over time.

I wish I could say this lesson was learned after this story, but I tell you this is one of my biggest slip ups. Even after half this book was written, I felt "distant" from God, but was doing all the things I felt I was supposed to be doing according to *my* plan. I asked God about this one day. His response to me was both loud and gentle, "Am I a God that must submit to the system?" He is bigger than the system we put Him in. I need to walk with Him, not my plan.

THE DECEPTION

What characteristic of God are you certain of? Most people will say love. I say love. It's what we're taught. Guess what? We are right! God is love. And He is also so much more! This is what we do with concepts like God. We try to simplify and explain it. God is painfully simple and powerfully complex at the same time. It doesn't take long to listen to sermons from any pastor to hear some sort of claim that "If we could do just one thing..." or "It all comes down to..." Again, these statements are our demise. The conviction in the moment is likely correct and, typically, if we follow through with whatever the pastor is asking for that season, there will be tremendous fruit. The problem comes when God keeps moving on and we keep living like God only cares about one thing.

I write all this because this very book you're reading outlines some specific topics and ideas that are helpful for Chrisitans finishing the race of life with a deep passion for the Lord. But I must caution us all: *our life will not equally reflect the habits and ideas in this book at all times.* Rather, it seems that God reveals Himself to us in waves. I can read the Bible in large portions for a while and it is so life-giving, then all of a sudden, it gets hard. Sometimes I can wake up early and pray and then during another season, it feels pointless. When I share the gospel, people come to salvation in bunches and then: nobody. If it were up to me, I should daily be reading, praying, evangelizing, operating in the miraculous, and loving my neighbor. Humans have made this stress to be well-rounded, not God. I meet a lot of burnt out Christians that feel like they aren't good enough because they aren't meeting all their Christian duties. Says who? Our standards or God's standards?

My deception looks like this: I read something or hear something from scripture and I say to myself, "If I could just do..." or "It all boils down to..." I have said this about dozens of different topics. It's all about love. It's all about grace. It's all about the fear of the Lord. It's all about truth. It's all about making disciples. It's all about loving the orphan and the widow. It's all about loving God and others. It's all about being generous. It's all about Jesus. It's all about the Holy Spirit. It's all about our Father in Heaven. It's all about the cross. Notice, none of these statements are false, but to say that one of these is more supreme than the other leaves me with a zoomed in view of God. It's very hard to *only* be about 12 different things at the same time. A healthier approach would be to say, "These are things God has shown me about His character and ways during my lifetime so far. I know they are true and I know He will keep showing me more of Himself."

I have written, "It's all about..." before each of those different statements and others in my lifetime, but what God is doing is beautifully teaching me the expanse of his wisdom and ways. Each one of those statements was a season of my life where God was drawing me closer to Him. He teaches me the reverence for Jesus, or the power of His Spirit, or the glory of the Father. He shows me

His heart for mankind and the blessedness of a generous heart. He shows me that He is not a God to be taken lightly, but can be approached with confidence due to His abounding love and mercy. My mind wants to simplify God into an equation. However, God doesn't seem to desire to belittle Himself for our finite minds to comprehend. Rather, He seems to desire to build on ideas, beliefs, and principles, so that He can draw our hearts more heavenward and towards His greatness.

We are hitting roadblocks of burnout because we have tried to explain God simply, and God is trying to prove to our minds that He is bigger. It's perspective. I have seen this many times in worship services. Someone will walk into a service with problems of any kind, and just a short time later at the end of the service, they say, "Everything has changed in my life."

Now let's think. What actually changed in an hour or two? Very little on earth changes in an hour especially when it comes to the complexities of human nature. You know what changes people in that amount of time? Their perspective. They walk into the service with a big problem and a small God, and they walk out with a small problem and a big God. Afterwards, they have a more proper view of God. Their problems felt bigger than life, and then they encountered a God who is bigger than their problems. All of a sudden, they are in a much better position because they see their life, sin, and issues against the backdrop of a big God. It reminds me of the old hymn lyrics:

> Turn your eyes upon Jesus.
> Look full, in his wonderful face.
> And the things of earth will grow strangely dim.
> In the light of his glory and grace.

We must realize God is bigger than the bad things and He is even bigger than the good things in our life. Maintaining a posture that recognizes God's omnipotence will do a good job of keeping us out of the ditches on both sides of the road regardless of the path at hand.

Our human minds love to whittle things down so we can tweet it, but I am saying even as I write a book to unveil The Rejuvenated Life, can we actually make God bigger, not smaller? Embrace the mystery. Embrace the complex. Embrace the beauty that there is a God and it isn't *you*.

To walk with God our whole lives, we have to be walking too. Whenever He moves, we do. We call our relationship with God a "walk," but then we get thrown off when God moves us to a new place either physically, emotionally, or spiritually. If our prayer time, quiet time, Bible study, evangelism, giving, serving, or any other thing that we pride our faith with God on isn't refreshing anymore, it's not because the practice is wrong. It's because God walked ahead to show us more and we didn't follow along.

A lot of the topics in this book will be helpful and provide immediate impact. But do not hold on to them so tightly that you make your life mantra about a certain practice. We are to be faithful to God, not the practices that lead us to God. It's the difference between burnout and the light and easy yoke that Christ offers. We want to worship God in the fullness of His glory here on earth. We do not want to make idols of the vehicles that lead us to a closer walk with God. Jesus didn't often go into the countryside to spend time with the Father because that's what a good Christian should do. He did it because he longed to spend time with the Father. Don't make this plan your God. Let God be God, and may we walk with Him daily.

I do not want The Rejuvenation Project to become a spiritual burden that ultimately leads more people into the very bondage it was designed to free them of. I am actively trying to embrace a simple principle: If my spiritual devotion with God has become laborious, it's probably because He moved on to show me more and I didn't follow. God's presence is what keeps life refreshing, not our spiritual striving. Where He is, peace and ease of mind will follow. Notice, I am not talking about peace and ease of *circumstance*. I am talking about our inner spirit. Even if the world around us is in turmoil, we can still be inwardly at ease if we are in His presence, plan, and purpose.

> And no one pours new wine into old wineskins. Otherwise, the new wine will burst the skins; the wine will run out and the wineskins will be ruined. No, new wine must be poured into new wineskins. And no one after drinking old wine wants the new, for they say, 'The old is better.' (Luke 5:37-39, NIV)

One of Jesus' first parables is about comparing and contrasting old and new wine. In the context of this parable, Jesus is talking to the religious leaders about fasting. This is a perfect example of receiving something for a season. Fasting is a great practice for walking with God, but the religious leaders had a higher view of fasting than actually realizing that God's son was in their presence.

> Jesus answered, 'Can you make the friends of the bridegroom fast while he is with them? But the time will come when the bridegroom will be taken from them; in those days they will fast.' (Luke 5:34-35, NIV)

Jesus doesn't diminish fasting. He is making a point that there is something better happening in that season than fasting. Jesus isn't making a statement of right or wrong. He is making a statement that *timing matters*. God wants to pour out new wine. He wants to give a fresh helping of Himself to us. We must not take the new things God is giving us and then put them into our old systems and patterns. We have to receive what God has for us in each season, fresh and new.

The last sentence of that parable is striking though. You would think that receiving new wine with new wineskins is the priority, but the reality is that the *old* wine is the best. God is giving us new wine and we have to receive it with new wineskins; not so we drink it, but rather, so it can sit and ferment and become good. When God shows us something about Himself and we come to a conclusion in that moment, it is like drinking fresh pressed wine. Sometimes, He reveals himself through years of mystery. Let's not rush to conclusions so we have great new advice to share. When God reveals something to us, and we receive it as true, we must also hold it in the context of a bigger God. That truth will ferment over our lifetime and we will reap a reward of wisdom and knowledge as we grow in years.

The contents of this book will either bring us life or death. If we read this book to try to define God and make Him fit into our system, we will wither. If we read this book with an understanding that God is bigger than the system and even more complex than the things we are even most certain of, He will bring life to our bones. Hold the plan lightly, hold God tightly.

THE REJUVENATION PROJECT

First, I'd like you to read Isaiah 40 with a desire to awe at the grandeur of God. After reading that passage, pray and repent of the times that you have tried to explain God and make Him simple rather than embrace the complexity and profoundness of God.

What quality of God are you most certain of? What spiritual discipline are you most certain a Christian should do? Whatever you answer, I challenge you to live without both of those for a short period. I am sure you are correct with your answers, but putting those two things on the back burner will expand the profound nature of God in your life.

Again, think about God building into you His ways and nature, and think of Him doing this in waves, not all at once. It may feel lopsided for a season, but ultimately, it is God who is expounding His ways in your life. We are building for our last day to be our best day, not today.

Here is an example: If someone would say that God is love and that a Christian has to read their Bible every day, I would encourage them to pray a prayer like this: *God I know you are love and that your Word is good, but I also know that you are bigger. Will you show me?* From there, I would then encourage them to use their time with God to do something different, like sit in solitude and dwell on the holiness or reverence of God, rather than continue in their usual patterns of reading and dwelling on God's love.

You will not live without these disciplines forever, but do try to live absent of your certainties for two or three weeks and you will begin to discover more of God than you thought was available. I give you permission to not be well-rounded in your faith today so that you can know more about how big our God is. I pray God expands your mind.

CHAPTER THREE

WASHED BY THE WORD

REMEMBER BEING IN Sunday school as a kid? The teacher would be teaching a lesson and then ask the kids how the lesson might be applied in their life. No matter what, there were two answers that guaranteed a pat on the back: "Jesus" or "The Bible." *"Johnny, what's the best way to follow Christ?"* "READ THE BIBLE!" *"Johnny, what are you going to eat for lunch today?"* "THE BIBLE!" *Teacher thinks to themselves, "I guess Jesus *did* say that man should not live on bread alone..." *"Very profound answer, Johnny!"*

For so many of us, the Bible or Jesus is still the obvious answer. We wrongly assume there is no way these glaringly clear answers can help us understand our complex lives and questions, so we look everywhere else for fulfillment and understanding. If we have deep problems, then we need to find deeper answers. Right? Not necessarily. I'd like us to look at the situation under a different light. Maybe the answer *is* obvious. Maybe God isn't trying to trick us after all.

Jesus makes a distinct statement in Mark 4:13, "Then Jesus said to them, 'Don't you understand this parable? How then will you understand any parable?'" (NIV). Bold statement. If we want to understand the Kingdom of God, we have to understand Jesus' teachings. A large portion of His teachings were in the form of parables: fictional stories used to convey heavenly principles. The meanings of some parables are clearer than others. Thankfully, Jesus makes it pretty clear where the starting point is for understanding His teachings. It's the Parable of the Sower. Jesus says that we have to understand this parable if we want to understand any of the rest, so let's concentrate on this passage. Take a read below from Mark 4:1-9:

> Again, Jesus began to teach by the lake. The crowd that gathered around him was so large that he got into a boat and sat in it out on the lake, while all the people were along the shore at the water's edge. He taught them many things by parables, and in his teaching said: "Listen! A farmer went out to sow his seed. As he was scattering the seed, some fell along the path, and the birds came and ate it up. Some fell on rocky places, where it did not have much soil. It sprang up quickly, because the soil was shallow. But when the sun came up, the plants were scorched, and they withered because they had no root. Other seed fell among thorns, which grew up and choked the plants, so that they did not bear grain. Still other seed fell on good soil. It came up, grew and produced a crop, some multiplying thirty, some sixty, some a hundred times. Then Jesus said, "Whoever has ears to hear, let them hear." (NIV)

Let's put ourselves in the crowd listening to Jesus that day. We are squinting out into the water and tuning our ears to a man we can't help but feel drawn to. He says, "Listen!" our hearts jump as we lean in to focus. We listen to the story and wonder where He is going with it. We comprehend that a farmer is planting crops and then he plants the crops in four types of soils. The soils determined what was produced from them, and then Jesus finishes by saying if we have ears that we should hear what He said.

If I am being honest, if I was in the crowd that day, I would think the parable was about a bad farmer that needed to pay more attention to where he was planting his crops. As the story goes, it's clear I am not the only one who was a little confused.

Later, Jesus' disciples asked for more info, so Jesus began to explain the parable to them. He prefaces his explanation by noting the importance of this parable specifically: *"Don't you understand this parable? How then will you understand any parable?"* (Mark 4:13, NIV). Thankfully, this is one of the few parables that Jesus gives us the explanation for. Here is the explanation straight from the man himself from Mark 4:14-20:

> The farmer sows the word. Some people are like seed along the path, where the word is sown. As soon as they hear it, Satan comes and takes away the word that was sown in them. Others, like seed sown on rocky places, hear the word and at once receive it with joy. But since they have no root, they last only a short time. When trouble or persecution comes because of the word, they quickly fall away. Still others, like seed sown among thorns, hear the word; but the worries of this life, the deceitfulness of wealth and the desires for other things come in and choke the word, making it unfruitful. Others, like seed sown on good soil, hear the word, accept it, and produce a crop—some thirty, some sixty, some a hundred times what was sown. (NIV)

Let's make some observations. The farmer (God) sows seed which represents the Word of God. The seed is the same no matter which type of soil it lands on. People's hearts are represented in the types of soil where the seed is sown, four types in all. Let's take a look into each of the soils below because that is our part in the process.

THE SOIL OF THE PATH

Back in Jesus' time, no paths were paved, but they were just as rock solid as their pavement counterparts of the future. If we were to plant any seed on these well-traveled paths, our best bet for growth would be for the seed to get kicked into the softer soil just off to the side. More likely to happen, the seed would get eaten by birds or other animals without a chance to grow. Jesus uses this soil to describe a person who hears the Word of God, but the Word is unable to touch that person's heart because it is so hard. Satan comes and takes away the Word before it ever has a chance to find the soft part of the heart.

The question I have is, "What makes a person's heart hard?" I'd say there is really one clear answer: *life*. Just like natural soil becomes hardened when it is uncultivated, so our hearts become hardened when we do not allow them to be touched. Life happens to everyone. It is the footprints of thousands of people walking innocently around you. After being stepped on so many times, we cope by becoming hardened rather than working to maintain a soft and open heart to others. In the natural realm, if I were to till a garden, the soil would be receptive to seeds and growth because there is space for the life to grow. If I tilled a garden and returned a couple years later, I would return to see that gravity and other natural forces had caused the soil to fill in all the open spaces. For new life to grow, there has to be space for it to occur. Hardness has no open space.

To bring this analogy to our actual hearts. Let's say something bad happens to us. We are prone to ignoring the issue, allowing a bad memory or circumstance to be pushed deep into our hearts over time. We cope by covering it with an emotional callous so as to forget the memory completely and prevent future pain from happening. This hardening of the heart certainly does keep more emotional pain from occurring, but it also prevents the heart from receiving anything good in the future. A hardened heart blocks both the good and the bad.

It doesn't matter what our circumstances have been, are, or will be; life naturally hardens our hearts. Most of the time, the hardening process is unnoticeable. If unchecked, our heart becomes hardened to a point that even the Word of God has no ability to impact it. Is this you? Likely not. If you have made it at least this far in the book, you probably have a heart that still has some desire to know God and know His Word. Your heart may not be the softest soil, but I pray there is still open space for God's Word to grow in your heart.

Cultivation of the heart to prevent hardening involves trust. It allows for the soil of our heart to be turned over regularly like the fields each spring so that nothing unwanted grows and the things we want to grow *will* grow. The truth is that there are numerous things that make a heart hard, but two acts of trust keep the soil of our heart soft. We will get to that a bit later in this chapter.

ROCKY SOIL

If you have ever planted grass, you will have noticed that grass can grow anywhere... for a time. I remember going out in my backyard and planting some grass one spring. The grass began to grow literally everywhere. I even saw a blade of grass growing on a small rock. There was just a little dirt caked on the rock, but it was enough for a blade of grass to begin to grow. In the dampness of spring, the exposed root was able to survive, but when I looked for the same grass in July, it was long gone. What happened? It died because the root was barely covered.

A plant is only as healthy as its roots. We love to awe at what is above ground, but it is what is below the ground that gives life. Jesus says in John 15:5, "I am the vine; you are the branches. If you remain in me and I in you, you will bear much fruit; apart from me you can do nothing" (NIV). Without the root, there is no life. The Word of God died in the hearts of the people represented as rocky soil because the environment of the heart was unable to sustain the Word of God.

I have seen this most accurately represented in life through camps and conferences. When rocky soil people go to an environment where the Spirit of God is at work, they respond just like everyone else. The problem is, when they go home, it all dies away. As Christians, sometimes we make it worse on these people because they express life change and we tell them their life has changed at the camp, retreat, or conference. We pump up their righteous ego and then send them home to die like grass in the heat of the summer sun. And they're worse off than before.

The Rocky soil is about environment. Are we stewarding an environment in our hearts that grows the Word of God? Initial growth, believe it or not, is *not* the goal. Sustained, fruitful growth is the metric of the Kingdom of God. The problem is, our churches and well-intentioned leaders have become so desperate for a "win" that we've jump-started growth without creating a continued environment to sustain that growth. Ultimately, these people abandon the Word of God when persecution comes.

For the people represented as the rocky soil, Jesus is great as long as He fits into their life. When repentance or standing out in the crowd comes, they will get rid of Jesus before they get rid of their life. Jesus never minces His word on this subject, "Whoever wants to be my disciple must deny themselves and take up their cross daily and follow me" (Luke 9:23, NIV). God is not okay to be second fiddle to anything or anyone. Once again, we cannot expect a fruitful life without giving God space to grow.

THORNY SOIL

The third type of soil is different from the first two. The first seed never germinates, the second seed *only* germinates, and the third seed is a full-fledged plant. How do we know this? Let's read the scripture again. "Still others, like seed sown among thorns, hear the word; but the worries of this life, the deceitfulness of wealth and the desires for other things come in and choke the word, making it unfruitful" (Mark 4:18-19, NIV). There is one word used to describe this category of soil specifically: *unfruitful.*

Every living thing was designed to reproduce. Literal human reproduction halts when a person, specifically a woman, doesn't have proper nutrition to carry a baby. For example, if a woman is starving on a desert island, her body has the wherewithal to know that reproducing a baby in the midst of starvation would be bad for all parties involved. Same is true of trees. If an apple tree lacks proper care and nutrients, the fruit production suffers before the tree comes close to completely dying.

Here is the point: Just because something is alive, doesn't mean it's fruitful. Even Jesus Himself once ran across a fig tree with no fruit and had some pointed words for it. "Seeing a fig tree by the road, he went up to it but found nothing on it except leaves. Then he said to it, 'May you never bear fruit again!' Immediately the tree withered" (Matthew 21:19, NIV). Yikes! Having fruit is a big deal to Jesus.

In Jesus' parable, the seed growing in thorns had done its best, but ultimately it was lacking fruit because the weeds around it were taking the vital nutrients needed for the plant to be fruitful. What is stealing our spiritual nutrients necessary to be fruitful? Jesus says it's the worries of this life, the deceitfulness of wealth, and the desires for other things.

To bring this into our everyday lives, when we lose focus of the true source of life, we will experience a long history of over-working and under-producing before we die. Our typical response to feeling our spiritual vibrancy slipping away is to work harder. The harder we try to be fruitful and work on our own strength, the more the worries of life and the deceitfulness of wealth and desires for other things take hold. We get into a vicious cycle until we just can't handle feeling depleted any longer. We quit. We burn out. We leave the thing we once felt called to. Why? Because we lost sight of our true source of nourishment.

This category of soil will be the most Christians who burn out. The first soil never becomes a Christian, the second soil is a Christian for a short amount of time, but the third soil is a large majority of life-long believers in Christ. We look the part, but never have anything to show. We work hard, but never see any fruit. We are in churches, but can never define if we are actually doing a good job. We are busy bodies. We celebrate the smallest of spiritual victories. We put in double the work for half of the reward. Most likely, we are just really tired. It goes unnoticed for a while because structurally, there is no difference between a fruitful plant and an unfruitful one. The support is there, there just isn't any fruit.

How can you tell if this is you? You might say things like, "It feels like I'm doing everything right, but I just don't have anything to show for it." The faith of this person is in themselves, and rarely ends well. In fact, since there is no fruit, they are just starving to death. I know, it's grim, but there is hope. We can be good soil.

THE GOOD SOIL

We may have felt convicted that our life is more reflected in one of the other soils, but I know we always hope to be the good soil. I mean, who wouldn't? How amazing is it that we can have one crop that doesn't just produce what is expected, but actually produces 30, 60 or 100 times more than what was anticipated? How much more amazing would it be if we could say the same thing about our lives? If the previous soil does double the work for half the reward, this person does half the work for double the reward.

What makes the good soil good? It's actually not that complex. Two things Jesus says: (1) hear the word and (2) accept it. That's it! There is no special fertilizer necessary. People that produce a crop well above their expectancy are the ones who hear God's Word and do what it says. They don't try harder; they just allow the Word to do what it does best without getting in the way.

It astonishes me how many people claim to build their whole life around God and yet have never even read the whole Bible. I get it, it's long. But eternal life is longer. Many of us have professed a faith in a gospel that we haven't even read or listened to completely. The entire Bible is the gospel - not just Matthew, Mark, Luke, and John. How can we understand the depths of God's love when we haven't even read everything God wants to reveal to us?

One of the greatest tips I can give someone who desires to live a complete life for the Lord is to just read or listen to the whole Bible. Notice I said, "read" and not "study." I am not knocking studying, but before we can really do a good study, we should just read the text. Just read it as if you were reading this book. You aren't dissecting why I chose a specific word; you are just taking in the message through the words I am writing.

The Bible is not your average book. Hebrews 4:12 says, "For the word of God is alive and active. Sharper than any double-edged sword, it penetrates even to dividing soul and spirit, joints and marrow; it judges the thoughts and attitudes of the heart" (NIV). The Bible is alive, which means there is always more flowing from within it. Sometimes I wish we didn't see the Bible as a book because there is no other book that is alive. Most of the time with a book, the first time reading it is the most life changing and enjoyable. But with the Bible, the *most recent* reading is the most life changing and enjoyable because it is alive and active. The worst time through the Bible, if I can use such a term, is the first because with each pass through the Bible, the scripture unveils more of who God is. We should eliminate the idea that we can learn and study everything about the Bible in one pass. We have to be lifelong consumers of the Word of God. Not so we can explain it, but so we can live it.

Rather than read the Word of God ourselves, many of us prefer and sometimes exclusively read or listen to other people's interpretations of the Bible. I am not saying that learning from others is bad, I am saying that learning from God directly is better. I'd rather eat my steak myself, not let someone else chew it for me. Relying exclusively on someone else's viewpoint of scripture is like letting someone else chew your food for you. That's not how I like to digest food.

Unfortunately, many people build their theological belief systems on other people's foundations and then wonder why it crumbles when the storms of life come. We each need a solid foundation in scripture. Sure, there are people that know more about the Bible than we do, but there is no substitution for getting the Word of God into our own hearts. That is why my suggestion to all is to first read the Bible without looking too hard under the surface for meaning. Let's just see what it says with our own eyes and hearts. This is the first step to getting the Word of God in our hearts. The Bible judges our hearts, we do not judge the Bible. There is no quick way to get the Bible in our heart. We have to start reading and listening to it regularly on our own and commit to this for a lifetime.

Many people who get true revelation from God's Word and are able to teach it or pass it along have read through the Bible at least a few times on their own before the teachings come out really fresh. God plays the long game. He isn't going to throw deep and true revelation to a person who is looking for a quick fix or who just randomly opens up the Bible to see what God says for that day. God isn't random. Just look around the world and creation. He seems to have a plan and His words to us are just as well thought out.

The reason we think the Bible is out of touch is because we haven't given our lives to reading it. Read it over and over and over. I have never met a person who said they wished they hadn't read the Bible as much. It is usually the opposite story. If we seek God, we will find Him. He didn't promise seeking would be easy, but He did say we will find Him. Just start reading! If we want to be good soil, we first have to hear the message.

The second thing that Jesus said determines whether soil is good or not is that we have to accept the Word. It is one thing to hear, it is another thing to accept. Many people have read the Bible, but few people live by it. What does accepting the Word mean? It means that whatever we read, we obey. The Bible is our rule of life. When we read something, we must simply say "If the Bible teaches it, I must live it." There is little room for personal opinions in the Word of God.

Accepting it is when we read a piece of scripture that challenges our heart and instead of throwing out the scripture, we throw out our feelings. It is choosing to believe and live by the principle that God's Word reigns supreme. John 1:1 settles the debate on the supremacy of God's word, "In the beginning was the Word, and the Word was with God, and the Word was God" (NIV). Just a few verses later, "The Word became flesh and made his dwelling among us. We have seen his glory, the glory of the one and only Son, who came from the Father, full of grace and truth" (John 1:14, NIV). Jesus is the Word. If we feel triggered by an approach that says God's Word reigns supreme, then we need to question whether Jesus is actually the Lord of our life. Jesus is the Way, the Truth, and the Life. He is everything and His Words are Him. If we discount God's Word, we discount Jesus as Lord of all.

Our world has no problem searching for truth, but we do have a hard time agreeing on what it is. If we were to debate the most recent hot topic in culture, we would probably start with a statement, "I think." This statement leads to division on so many levels. Across the board, Christian or not, there is agreement that there is a line of good and evil. The debate is over where that line is. If we have 8 billion people and each has a different line for good and evil, we can understand why our world can be in such turmoil. Accepting the word of God means that instead of spelling out our world view with, "I think," we start with "Jesus teaches." Accepting the Word is to accept God's line in the sand whatever it may be. Understandably, that line may still feel unclear when we cast the words of scripture on a modern culture, but rest assured, the guidance is there if we give our lives to hearing and accepting the Word of God.

Hearing or reading the Word of God is not usually the problem. It's the *accepting* part that trips us up. It's not very popular to start out an argument using, "The Bible says." Be prepared for nobody to listen to you after that. Just live it out anyway. We don't read the Bible so we are educated. We read to be transformed into the likeness of Christ. Don't worry about how people react initially to a world view through scripture. Overtime people will start asking us how we live when we have a crop of 30, 60, or 100 times what was sown and they have little to no fruit to show.

Which soil are you? It's really your choice. Earlier in the book, we had to decide that God is good, and now we have to choose that God's Word is good by hearing and accepting what it says. That choice makes us good soil. I have yet to meet a man or woman fully surrendered to the Word of God who hates their life. I urge every reader: hear and accept God's Word so that the world can see what God can do through a man or woman fully surrendered to Him.

LET IT GROW

After the Parable of the Sower, Jesus tells another parable about seed in Mark 4:26-29:

> He also said, "This is what the kingdom of God is like. A man scatters seed on the ground. Night and day, whether he sleeps or gets up, the seed sprouts and grows, though he does not know how. All by itself the soil produces grain—first the stalk, then the head, then the full kernel in the head. As soon as the grain is ripe, he puts the sickle to it, because the harvest has come." (NIV)

Again, contextually in the teaching the seed is the Word of God. Once we decide to hear and accept the Word of God, our job is to fill our heart with God's Word. We must become obsessed with reading it and sowing it into our hearts. However, do not expect a harvest right away. As we put the word of God in our heart, it grows. Night and day, whether we think about it or not, it grows. Finally, it produces fruit in our life after a period of time. The longer the wait, the more valuable the harvest.

Let's think more about agriculture. What's the first thing we need to grow a plant? Seed. What's the end product of that plant? Fruit with a lot more of the same seeds. The thing we plant ends up being reproduced exactly with the proper care and time. The same is true with the Word of God. We plant it in our hearts by reading and listening to it, and then we accept it and it grows. Eventually, what will begin to come out of our hearts is exactly what we put in. "For the mouth speaks what the heart is full of" (Luke 6:45, ESV). The end product of a life devoted to the Bible is that we are transformed to speak the very words of God out of our own hearts rather than the sinful thoughts we are accustomed to. This is how we live like Jesus. Put wisdom in, let it grow, and eventually godly wisdom will flow from within us. Now *that's* the fruit I am hoping for in my life.

Jesus' next parable is the Parable of the Mustard Seed. It's the smallest plant, but grows to be the largest of the garden plants (Mark 4:30-32). Why does that matter? Because when we start reading scripture, we needn't start big or expect a harvest immediately. We must be content to start small.

When I was in 6th grade, I decided to start reading the Bible by my own choice. I started by reading two chapters a day. After I finished a book of the Bible, I would underline that book in the table of contents so I could keep track of what I'd read. I kept going, chapter by chapter, book by book, until I finished the whole Bible. Then, I started over. On and on, again and again. I repeated this pattern for many years. I believe the fruit of the book you're reading right now is entirely because of that very pattern: time spent in God's word, slowly but surely. Now, over a decade later, I am still reaping that harvest of faithfulness to God's word while continually sowing more of the Word in my heart.

When we start out reading, it can be difficult because we don't always have a lot to show for it early on. But later on, it produces a harvest. I know we have big dreams, but we must start small. No matter what your relationship with the Bible is right now, make a commitment to prioritize it in your life. Become a little more faithful to the scriptures each day and your life will be changed.

FREEDOM FROM SIN

John 6:66 describes that even Jesus had a bad day of ministry by human standards, "From this time many of his disciples turned back and no longer followed him" (NIV). We are accustomed to hearing a narrative of Jesus who accepted all people. Jesus does accept all people, but that doesn't mean people accept Him back. What could Jesus say that would cause so many to disregard him? Let's look at John 6:53-58.

> Jesus said to them, "Very truly I tell you, unless you eat the flesh of the Son of Man and drink his blood, you have no life in you. Whoever eats my flesh and drinks my blood has eternal life, and I will raise them up at the last

> day. For my flesh is real food and my blood is real drink. Whoever eats my flesh and drinks my blood remains in me, and I in them. Just as the living Father sent me and I live because of the Father, so the one who feeds on me will live because of me. This is the bread that came down from heaven. Your ancestors ate manna and died, but whoever feeds on this bread will live forever." (NIV)

I can't necessarily fault those who turned away from Jesus after this. Afterall, this sounds more like the start of a zombie cult than a redemptive plan for humanity. Was Jesus literally telling us to eat His flesh and drink His blood? There is absolutely no indication this is what Jesus meant. So, what does it mean to drink His blood and eat His flesh?

Blood is significant because it is necessary for the atonement of sin. The punishment for sin is eternal death (Romans 3:23). Without a sacrifice with blood there is no forgiveness of sins. Hebrews 9:22 says, "In fact, the law requires that nearly everything be cleansed with blood, and without the shedding of blood there is no forgiveness" (NIV). When Jesus poured out His blood on calvary, He was atoning for the sins of the world, once for all. To drink His blood is to receive the sacrifice that was poured out for our sins. Praise God!

I am so thankful for Jesus' sacrifice for me. However, you may be like me. After I surrendered my life to Jesus and allowed the blood of Jesus to wash me white as snow, my desire to sin didn't seem to get washed away too. I believed that God separated me from my sins as far as the east is from the west, but it also seemed like my sin kept staring me in the face. If God had this great plan of redemption, why do I and so many other born again Christians still struggle with sins daily?

The answer is in the flesh. We must drink His blood *and* eat His flesh. Remember John 1:14, "The word became flesh..." What is the flesh of Christ? It's the Word of God. It's the Bible! Jesus and His Word are not just the answer for having forgiveness of sins, but also living sinless. Let's also look at Ephesians 5:25-27.

> Husbands, love your wives, just as Christ loved the church and gave himself up for her to make her holy, cleansing her by the washing with water through the word, and to present her to himself as a radiant church, without stain or wrinkle or any other blemish, but holy and blameless. (NIV)

At first glance, this passage seems to be addressed to husbands. But let's forget about husbands for a second and look at the example that Paul is asking husbands to follow. Paul is asking husbands to follow in the example of Christ's love for us. This is how He loves us: He "gave himself up for *us* to make *us* holy, cleansing *us* by the washing with water through the word, and to present *us* to himself as a radiant church, without stain or wrinkle or any other blemish, but holy and blameless."[3] God's plan was never for us to sulk in our sins for our whole lives with no hope of getting free. He always planned for us to be presented to Himself "without stain or wrinkle or any other blemish, but holy and blameless." Let's hear and accept this. God's plan is for us to be pure and holy. He accomplishes this through the blood on the cross to atone for our sins and then He uses the Word to wash us clean. This is the power of the blood and flesh of Christ. Jesus really is the antidote for sin whether in the past or for those we currently battle. For the latter, there is more than a simple prayer of salvation involved.

Deep down in each of our hearts is gunk. Everyone has their dark hidden sins. What we like to do is push those dark sins way down deep in our hearts so that nobody can ever see them. Sometimes we are so good at pushing them deep down that we even forget about them ourselves! But the problem is that, no matter how deep down we push our sins, they are still within us.

Picture a cup with dirty black engine oil in the bottom of it. Gross, yeah. This oil represents our sins. The task is for us to get the cup clean without tipping it over (or should I say, "kicking the bucket"). How do we get pure and holy while staying alive on earth? Well, most of us see the dirty oil in the bottom of the cup and stick our fingers in to get it out. We try to be righteous by our own power. We will naturally remove some of the oil, but it leaves us messy and there will always be some oil that slips through our fingers. On our own power, sin will always be there. We may have less, but we will always be dirty. So how do we make the cup absolutely clean? We wash it with water. As we pour water into the glass that has oil at the bottom, the oil begins to come to the surface because water is more dense than oil. As we continually pour more water in, the oil comes closer to the surface because the water forces it out. Eventually, if we continue to pour in the water, the oil will be long gone and the cup will be full of pure water. This is what Jesus does to our hearts. He washes us with water through the *Word*.

The difficult teaching that caused so many to desert Jesus right in front of Him was the basic elementary Sunday School answer for God's redemptive plan for humanity. Who paid the price for our sin with His blood? Jesus. How does He continually make us holy and blameless? The Bible. When we consume the Bible, we are consuming the flesh of Christ. This scripture to drink the blood and eat the flesh is not just a reference to the sacrament of communion, it is the mode for freedom from sin and death.

The Bible is the ticket to freedom from that nagging sin that has walked with us our whole lives. As we hear and accept the Word of God, the deep hidden sins will be brought to the surface. As long as we keep pouring in the water through the Word, we will walk towards true freedom. Psalm 119:9 says, "How can a young person stay on the path of purity? By living according to your word" (NIV). Jesus adds in John 15:3, "You are already clean because of the word I have spoken to you" (NIV). God didn't hide his plan for us to be free from sin. He placed it right in front of our eyes and on most of our nightstands. God never intended for us to wallow in our sin until we die or Jesus returns. He plans to save us and clean us and both come from Jesus. We need to accept both into our lives.

THE REJUVENATION PROJECT

Decide today that you are going to live in the supremacy of God's Word. Surrender to the Lordship of Jesus Christ. He is the Word. Decide today to commit to hearing God's Word and accepting all of it. If you have not read the entire Bible, that is your first step. The more you read, the cleaner your heart will be.

If you have never been washed by the Word, I ask you to commit to reading the gospels, Matthew, Mark, Luke and John, every week for a month. That is about 12-13 chapters a day. From there, I encourage you to read the rest of the Bible. I have noticed from my life and others that a good daily washing is about 4-10 chapters a day. That is not a scientific number, just my observation. I am certain that reading the verse of the day just doesn't do much for the heart if we really want to live the life God is calling us to live. We've got to give our life to hearing and accepting the Word of God into our hearts.

If you are just starting out reading the Bible or are stuck in a rut of Bible reading, try to read large chunks in one sitting. Don't try to do a study on each word; just read it as fast as you can. You will be surprised how much more you are able to connect from different parts of the Bible when you do this.[4] Ultimately, my encouragement is to always read the Bible, but vary the pace of reading at different times in your life. Sometimes you need a power washer and sometimes you need a shower. Other times, you just need to wash your hands. Mixing up your pace and style of reading offers a new opportunity to put the Word of God into your heart and let it wash over you.

Friends, don't try to take in the whole Word with one pass through it: read it and let it wash you and let the Holy Spirit do the revealing over a lifetime. If something is confusing make a note and read on. You may find your answer as you keep reading. If something puts you in awe of God and you sense His presence, just stop reading and live in the power of the Word of God at that moment. You do not need a seminary degree to read the Bible. The

Bible is God's plan for making you whole and clean in this life. Do not ignore it.

Another thing to note: as you read the Bible more than you ever have, you may notice the immediate effects are amazing. It brings life to your heart. This is good! Soak it in. You will eventually find that this wears off and you may even find yourself struggling more with certain sins than you had previously. This is when people give up and slip back to their old ways. After all, it is pretty discouraging when you put more effort into God's Word just to turn around and be sinning more. But let's remember the big picture. The Word is washing the gunk out of your life and bringing it to the surface. When you feel sinful, it is actually God showing you where he is cleaning you! Press on by doubling down on reading the Word and repent of the sin at the surface. Don't try to push the sin back down deep in your heart where it was, but rather let it bubble on out of your heart. You are not under a spiritual attack of the devil. Your loving Father is cleaning your heart.[5]

When the sins surface as you are letting the Word wash you, just press on by reading and be thankful to Jesus because he is making you pure and holy. If you have never been washed by the Word, commit to 6 months of daily reading and listening to the Bible in larger sections than you ever have before. Don't try to comprehend it all, just read it and let it wash you. It may be hard for those 6 months, but if you are aware that the Word is washing you and that God is actually bringing your sins to the surface, you can humbly surrender your life even more to God and walk in the freedom that He gives. Go ahead and start reading and listening to the Bible[6] and commit to being a lifelong consumer of God's Word. You are made to be good soil.

CHAPTER FOUR

THE GOD COMPANY

AT SOME POINT in your life, you might have been asked, "When you get to heaven, what's the first thing you are going to ask God?" Or, when we don't understand something, many of us have thought, "I'll have to ask God when I see Him someday." For the most part, this question and thought is rooted in pure intentions, but it saddens me that many of us have a tendency to think of God simply as the ultimate search engine. Oftentimes, we spend more time looking for answers about God than we do actually getting to know Him ourselves. Without knowing God, there is little we can truly understand.

Now, we can only know God to the extent at which He has revealed Himself. He has hidden some things from us while at the same time revealing other things to us. And here's what we are to remember: *We are only responsible for what He has revealed to us.* Deuteronomy 29:29 says, "The secret things belong to the Lord our God, but the things revealed belong to us and to our children forever, that we may follow all the words of this law" (NIV). God may reveal the answer to some of our questions or He may not. That's not really up to us. However, let's not just give up right there.

I have never known God to be stingy, so the truth is, He likely wants to reveal more of the "secret things" to us than we think. Our focus in this quest for truth should not be in what is hidden, but the One who reveals it. A singular desire to know God, will lead to an understanding of the many secrets of life. To say it another way, the more we know God, the more we understand everything else.

Therefore, the question that should take top precedence in our life is "Who is God?" Notice, the question isn't, "Is there a God?" We have already established by faith that He exists and He is good and big. Now we start to fill in a clearer picture of who this God is. The question "Who is God?" acknowledges His presence, and seeks to know His heart. Ecclesiastes 3:11 says, "He has also set eternity in the human heart; yet no one can fathom what God has done from beginning to end" (NIV). It is set in our hearts that there is something more to this life than us. That's why many of us often acknowledge God, but that doesn't mean we know Him. Many are aware there is a God, but few pursue knowing Him. I pray you are one who seeks not just to know there is a God, but to actually know Him personally. To start understanding the question "Who is God?", let's start at the beginning.

Genesis 1:26 says, "Then God said, 'Let us make mankind in our image, in our likeness, so that they may rule over the fish in the sea and the birds in the sky, over the livestock and all the wild animals, and over all the creatures that move along the ground'" (NIV). We are made in the image of God. So, what does this mean? This means that we are called to replicate something greater than ourselves.

Currently in our postmodern society, many of us define truth based on each individual person's point of reference. It's not uncommon to hear qualifiers such as, "My truth." or "My personal belief." It sounds lovely in theory - this melting pot of morals - but the more we search our hearts for answers and truth, the more confused we seem to get. Why? Because the answers to our identity questions are not found by examining the deep unexplored areas of our hearts and minds. They're found in God's. When I have a clearer picture of God's image, I have a clearer picture of me. Let's get the gaze off of us and let's get it on Him. *It's vital we know who God is.*

A distinct characteristic about God is found in the word He uses to describe whose image and likeness we are made in. "Let *us* make mankind in *our* image, in *our* likeness..." It doesn't take much to understand that a word like *our* is plural, meaning more than one. How many likenesses are we made in? I do not wish to write a theological book, but we cannot live this life to the fullest and run the complete race of life well if we do not understand the image in which we are made. God is one and three at the same time: God the Father, God the Son, and God the Holy Spirit. This is mind-boggling for every human in existence, so why would God offer us such complicated math? He didn't do it to be confusing, He is showing us our ultimate destination.

Has someone ever questioned your personality or physical characteristics? "Why are you so outgoing?" "Why are you so competitive?" "I don't understand why you're so unorganized." "How did you get your red hair?" You can fill in your own questions that people ask you. These are difficult questions to answer because it's often just the way God made us. There are some things about our personalities we can control, but often the greatest God-given personality traits are so intertwined in our being that we couldn't change even if we wanted to. Often the only response to such questions is to say, "It's just the way I am."

It is just as insulting to question why God is the way He is. When many of us first truly contemplate the Holy Trinity, our gut reaction is often, "Why does it have to be so confusing?" It's like we are shaming God for being the way that He is. Existing three and one is not a public relations stunt to be confusing, but rather it's the essence of who He is and how He has made us. In the words of God himself, "I am who I am" (Exodus 3:14, NIV). Rather than question why God is the way He is, we need to just know Him for who He is.

God has never been alone. He has always been in relationship. Why would God make human beings? Because He *is* relationship. He loves being with others. The image that we are created in is relationship. It's the image of love. The image of closeness. The image of intimacy. It's the image of God. We are made for Him alone. That's it. Any identity or belief that goes beyond the fact that we were made for Him is a false identity or belief. We can certainly argue with that if we like, but if we do, we will also get burnt out and struggle with our purpose in life because we will try to make ourselves something we were never made to be. How peaceful it is to know that our image wasn't for doing, it was for being. Afterall, we are human beings, not human doings. Relationships are about being with one another. A relationship is the pinnacle of God's image and thus our image.

Relationships are more than just romance. We have friendships, family relationships, co-worker relationships, as well as our traditional romantic relationships. The idea behind all of these beautiful relationships is the opportunity to see others and be seen by others as we really are. Many of us have had good relationships with people and bad relationships with others. For the sake of our topic today, we must put any relational negativity behind us and imagine a relationship in its purest form. Even if we can picture true and pure relationships of all kinds, it is no less difficult for a finite mind to comprehend an eternal God. Thankfully, God himself has given examples for us to begin to see the way He is. Let's start by thinking about parents.

We all have parents. Maybe not all good parents, but we do have parents. Nobody gets here without them. We may know our biological parents or we may not. We may know one and not the other, but for the sake of the picture God has given us, let's imagine parents the way they were designed to be. For some reason, God made it necessary to have a man and a woman to have "relations" in order to create another human being. Everyone in existence has two biological parents, but which one is genetically more your parent? Is our biological mother or our biological father more our parent? One is not more biologically our parent than the other. We are equally both of them! Even though our biological parents are both equally our parents, we also understand that they are both distinctly different.

I had the pleasure of growing up with both of my biological parents in the same household. I can tell you that both my mom and dad are equally my parents, but I did not relate to them equally in all areas. Early in my life, I spent much more time with my mother. Later in life, I spend much more time with my father. If I wanted to spend the night at someone's house, I would go ask my mother. If I needed help fixing my car, I'd go to my father. If I felt sick, I'd find my mother. If I wanted to know who won the Cubs game, I'd go to my father. You get the gist. They are both equally my parents, but I interacted with them differently. Despite our earthly parental situation, this is a picture God is giving us for Himself.

There is God the Father, Son, and Holy Spirit, and even though they are all equally God, they are distinctly different. Most Christians have a tendency to approach just one person of God. A lot of us start our prayers to either the Father, Jesus or the Holy Spirit and always pray to the same person of God. Many churches emphasize the relationship with the Father and how we are nothing without Him. (Rightly so.) Other churches emphasize Jesus and how we are nothing without Him. (Rightly so.) Still other churches emphasize the Holy Spirit and that we are nothing without Him. (Again, rightly so.) So, which is right? Even though most Christian churches discuss all three, still more rely heavily on just one. Should this be the case? Isn't life better when we have both of our parents available to us? How much richer would life be if we interacted with all of our God the way He intended? We cannot know just part of Him; we have to know all.

In June of 2019, I had a dream. In my dream, I was sitting in a large church auditorium. I was in attendance at a church service with roughly 5,000 other people. I was sitting in the balcony of the auditorium high above the stage. My dream started right at the end of the service. I stood up with the thousands of others as the service came to a close. And although the dream had just started, I already had the context that Jesus was there. I stood up alongside my wife and I said, "Jesus is here, we have to go see Him!" We both immediately rushed out of the auditorium to make our way down the stairs to get to the bottom level. We knew that Jesus was available for us to see Him and talk to Him, but we also understood in the context of the dream that He wouldn't be there forever because He had other places to go.

I quickly found the greeting line for Jesus far out into the lobby of the church. As I waited, I noticed the line in front of me had many people, roughly 150 people in line before I was even in the auditorium. I noticed the line was moving relatively quickly, but the immediate 50 people in front of me weren't moving even though the line was. They just stood and talked to each other and got so absorbed in their conversations that they forgot they were in line to see Jesus. I yelled at them to keep moving, but they were so distracted that they couldn't hear me. So, with urgency, I decided to cut around them.

As I entered the doors of the auditorium, the vastness of the auditorium hadn't opened up yet. (Picture walking into a movie theater in the dark hallway before entering the big part of the room.) I walked in line down the hallway leading to the open auditorium only to be stopped by a female usher just before entering the big portion of the room where I would certainly get a glimpse of Jesus. The usher announced to everyone that Jesus' time was becoming limited and that she had to cut off the line to see Him. She told everyone else that they could get in the shorter lines to see the pastor or the worship band, but the Jesus line was too full tonight. I was unfortunately behind the cut off line. My heart sank. I had wanted to see Jesus so badly. In my frustration and desperation, I yelled very loudly over the line of people ahead of me towards the usher, "I don't want to see the pastor! I don't want to see the band! I want to see Jesus!" I braced myself to get scolded, but to my amazement, the usher gently smiled back and in a very normal tone said, "Okay! You can be the last in line to see Jesus."

She motioned me ahead of the others who were in line and made the cut off after me. I couldn't believe she allowed me to cut the other people. My heart was racing after all the emotion I felt, but finally, I knew I was going to see Jesus. After making the jump in line, I was now able to look around the massive auditorium. There were still hundreds of people in the room mingling after the service. I knew that I would have a view of Jesus at this moment. I quickly gazed around at different men in the crowd wondering, "Is that Jesus?" Finally, my eyes fixed on a young man. I caught a glimpse of him off to his side from a few hundred feet away and so I couldn't see him directly, but in my heart, I knew it was him. He was standing at the center of the stage talking to those who were gathered around him. I desperately wished to know what he was saying. His arms were stretched out wide like he was about to give a hug or show how he hung on a cross as he made his point to those in his vicinity. My heart was beating out of my chest! I was going to meet Jesus! And then I woke up.

I was amazed at my dream. I knew it was significant and from God, so I got up in the middle of the night and went to the living room and immediately wrote down everything I remembered. And then, I went back to sleep.

As soon as I went to sleep, I was back. I was standing in the exact same spot in the auditorium waiting to see Jesus. This time was different, though. Walking up behind Jesus now was a much taller and more powerful looking man. As he walked from the back of the stage where it was dimly lit to the center stage behind Jesus, I knew that this was Jesus' Father. As soon as my mind recognized this reality, I remember falling over faint and feeling pressed into the floor with such a great weight. I instantly woke up with a feeling of being pressed down upon in my bed. The weight of the glory of God! I recorded all these things in my journal, but was still puzzled by the dream and its profound nature that it had on my heart.

Months later, God showed me that my dream represents how God interacts with us. The usher was the Holy Spirit who made a way for me to see Jesus when there was no way to get to Him. Jesus had his arms open to the countless souls in the room. As they looked to Him, the Father was seen just behind him and exuded tremendous power and authority. The Holy Spirit was the way to Jesus and Jesus was the way to the Father.

John 14 is a powerful chapter of the Bible when it comes to the search of who God is and how He exists in three distinct persons. John 14:26 says, "But the Advocate, the Holy Spirit, whom the Father will send in my name, will teach you all things and will remind you of everything I have said to you" (NIV). The Holy Spirit is sent by the Father in the name of Jesus and will lead us in the ways of Jesus. Jesus initiates the sending of the Holy Spirit by asking the Father, "And I will ask the Father, and he will give you another advocate to help you and be with you forever—the Spirit of truth" (John 14:16-17, NIV). In John 14:6, Jesus says, "I am the way and the truth and the life. No one comes to the Father except through me. If you really know me, you will know my Father as well. From now on, you do know him and have seen him" (NIV).

In one chapter, Jesus acknowledges the distinctions in the Trinity, while also acknowledging how little is different. It's like they are three *and* one. We can recognize through Jesus' words that the Father sends the Holy Spirit and the Holy Spirit teaches us about Jesus, and Jesus leads us to the Father and asks the Father to send the Spirit. It may look like this on paper:

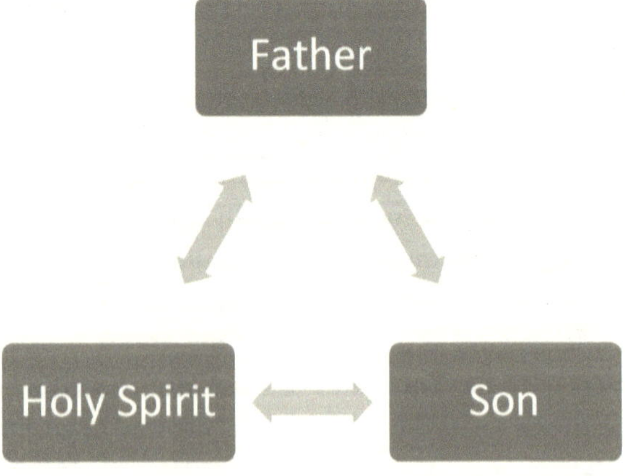

In this one act of sending the Holy Spirit, all three have a main role: the Holy Spirit for being sent, the Father for sending the Holy Spirit, and Jesus for initiating it all. This is just one moment of many. The cycle never ends and can also go in all directions. For instance, Jesus says that He came from the Father (John 16:28). In John 20:22, Jesus breathes on the disciples and says, "Receive the Holy Spirit." And in John 14:9, Jesus says, "Anyone who has seen me has seen the Father" (NIV). So, when the Holy Spirit teaches about Jesus, He is also revealing the Father. The God Company interacts with each other all through the scriptures and both sides of eternity. So, who is the most important person of the Trinity? That cannot be answered because God ceases to exist if one part is missing. Nothing happens without all of them.

The more we try to make the Trinity distinct, the more it seems to mesh together. There is no way to distinctly separate the Godhead. And that's exactly the type of relationship God wants with us. What if it were said of us that no one could tell the difference between God and us? He is inviting us into this type of relationship. A relationship with God in which we don't know where one starts and where the other ends. A relationship in which we are a distinct person, but are also completely engulfed in the heart of God. Like this:

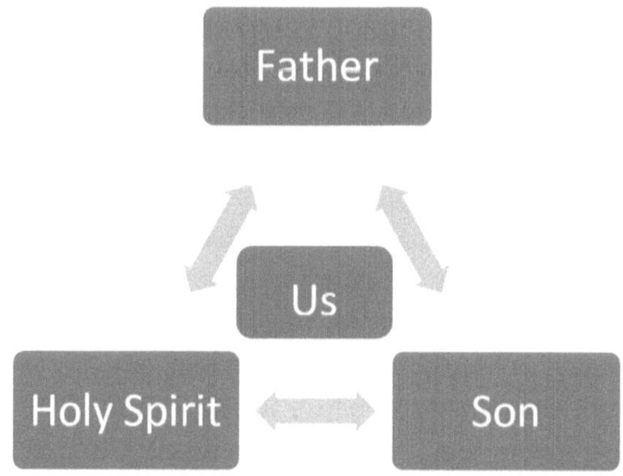

What we have to understand is that the Trinity is not a confusing theological principle, but rather, *it is our destination*. It is heaven. What is heaven without God? Our life is made to be with God. Not just part of Him, all of Him. We have to know who God is. I cannot tell us everything about God in one chapter, but I do wish we could all understand this one thing: don't limit Him. Get to know all of them. I want us to know what the voice of the Father sounds like. I want us to know Jesus' love and kindness. I want us to be in the presence of the Holy Spirit and adapt to His promptings. Quest to know all of God. I do not bring up this subject as somebody who has already succeeded in knowing God. I am no expert, but I am in pursuit. I urge you to join me in this pursuit.

For some, these ideas may have provoked offense. If not, just move on from this paragraph. If you feel offended, just understand that the Father, Jesus and the Holy Spirit are not offended by each other. They are not asking each other, "Why did Caleb pray to you and not to me?" Why is the Holy Spirit welcomed here, but not me?" There is no offense in God. He is pleased at being in relationship with us and especially when it is with all of Him. God understands our limits, but also calls us to live outside them through Him.

THE REJUVENATION PROJECT

A great way to start your search of knowing God is to begin to pray prayers addressed specifically to the Father, Jesus, or Holy Spirit. When you pray and when you read the scripture, ask yourself which part of the God Company is at work at that moment. Spend time praying to the Holy Spirit, then pray to the Father, and then spend time praying to Jesus. Picture them in your mind.

If you have a concern in your life, read scripture to figure out which person you should pray to. You cannot mess this up. It's not a trick. Jesus says in Matthew 7:9-11, "Which of you, if your son asks for bread, will give him a stone? Or if he asks for a fish, will give him a snake? If you, then, though you are evil, know how to give good gifts to your children, how much more will your Father in heaven give good gifts to those who ask him!" (NIV). He won't punish you for messing up. Instead, He may show Himself even more to you.

He desires a relationship with you. He isn't going to wipe you out anytime you pray to Jesus when it should have been to the Holy Spirit. This may seem impossible at first, but don't surrender to a life of vaguely knowing who God is. Be in constant pursuit, and take the leap of faith. As you begin to know all of God, you will also begin to understand all of you. And who knows, as you are more specific in your prayers, maybe you will begin to see more things happen through them.

CHAPTER FIVE

PRESENCE

AS WE CONTINUE to build the foundations of a rejuvenated life, let's now take a look at Jesus' very last few phrases before He ascended into heaven. "Therefore, go and make disciples of all nations, baptizing them in the name of the Father and of the Son and of the Holy Spirit, and teaching them to obey everything I have commanded you. And surely I am with you always, to the very end of the age" (Matthew 28:19-20, NIV). Jesus speaks His last words on earth as part of the "Great Commission," where - on a mountain in Galilee - He called on His followers to take the good news of the gospel to the ends of the earth.

The Great Commission is one of the most powerful mission focuses of scripture. Whenever I read these verses, I see focused action steps to carry out the work of the Lord Jesus Christ - to make disciples, to baptize, and to teach. But you know what part of the Great Commission I typically overlook? The last part. The very last promise Jesus left us with: that He is with us *always*. Oh how I wish this were the part of the Great Commission that we fixated on. No matter how hard we try, we will never be able to carry out the full work of our Lord Jesus without this last promise. In fact, if we want to carry out the Great Commission, we will be able to do that *only* to the level that we acknowledge and invite the presence of God into our lives.

God can do more in a second than man can do in a lifetime, and yet we toil in the work of God because we have removed Him from His own plans. Absolutely, unequivocally the presence of God is the game changer of life and the gateway to effectively carrying out the purpose God has given us. Presence is proximity. Nearness, closeness, *God with us*. He is with us whether we realize it or not. He is with us when we are feeling tremendous joy or extensive grief. He is with us in the midst of worshiping with thousands or being alone in tears. He is with us whether we acknowledge Him or curse Him. The Rejuvenated Life will come when we acknowledge His presence and understand that His presence is not just a means to an end goal, but the end goal itself.

When it comes to understanding what it means to be in God's presence, we first have to ask, "Where is God?" Don't overthink it. He is everywhere. We call it omnipresence. He is present everywhere all the time. That's a big God. King David says it like this: "Where can I go from your Spirit? Where can I flee from your presence? If I go up to the heavens, you are there; if I make my bed in the depths, you are there. If I rise on the wings of the dawn, if I settle on the far side of the sea, even there your hand will guide me, your right hand will hold me fast" (Psalm 139:7-10, NIV). As the familiar creepy Christmas song about Santa Claus goes, "He sees you when you're sleeping. He knows when you're awake." Except we aren't talking about a myth. We are speaking of the reality of God. And any reality that does not acknowledge that God is in our midst will lead to a life that falls short of the fullness He intended for us.

Since we randomly jumped into the Christmas spirit, let's remember the Christmas story from scripture. "The virgin will conceive and give birth to a son, and they will call him Immanuel" (which means "God with us") (Matthew 1:23, NIV). In reading the book of Matthew, the first thing we read about Jesus is that He will save us from our sins. The next thing? "He will be called Immanuel which means God with us." God is not someone that has to be summoned to be with us. He already *is*. There is a song we sing in church that has this line, "Holy Spirit you are welcome here." I don't have a problem with the song. In fact, I do love to sing it! But we don't have to welcome the Holy Spirit so that He shows up. We welcome the Holy Spirit to acknowledge that *He has always been here.* When we fail to understand that, we fall victim to the trappings of deism, which is the belief in the existence of a creator, but not as a supernatural deity who interacts with humankind.

Many of us may not express deism with our mouths, but a lot of us believe it in our hearts. We feel like God is distant. Like He's mad at us, or disappointed in us, or walking away as He shakes His head at another one of our mishaps or stumbles. However, even as we read this book, He is with us. Whether we're experiencing the best day of our life or the worst day of our life, God's presence doesn't change based on how we feel. Whether we feel God in our midst or feel He is the most distant, He has never changed His proximity to us. God has never been further from us or closer to us than He is right now.

Oftentimes, we get mixed up on this truth. Religion makes us feel like our likeability, our work, or our behavior is what draws the God of the universe closer to our daily lives. We question how worthy we are of God's presence when we ask questions like, "Did I pray long enough or good enough?" or have thoughts like, "I haven't desired to read my Bible in months, I must be distant from God." But the truth is, we can all experience the feeling of close proximity to God the moment we remember that there is nothing we can do to make Him come to us. He is near to us because He wants to be, not because we earned it.

I used to think the presence of God was very fragile. That I had to act just a certain way. Pray the right thing at the right time. Make sure I hadn't sinned in a few days, and then maybe I would experience the presence of God. But if I lost focus for a couple seconds or had a bad thought, He would run away again and make me start all over. *Lies.* God is near to me. He is near to you. And the quickest way to experience that nearness is also one of the simplest: say "thank you." Say it now even under your breath; feel the peace flood your heart and mind. It's like electricity. Gratitude is the plug that keeps us connected to the presence of God, and that connection sparks everything else. Just like electricity, even if we aren't plugged in, the current is still running, pulsing, strengthening - right next to us. A thankful heart is our connection to the real and tangible presence of God. When we feel distant from God, it isn't because God moved away. It's because our heart moved away from Him believing in our own self-sufficiency and neglecting to cultivate a thankful heart.

Paul says, "Do not be anxious about anything, but in every situation, by prayer and petition, *with thanksgiving*, present your requests to God. And the peace of God, which transcends all understanding, will guard your hearts and your minds in Christ Jesus" (Philippians 4:6-7, NIV). The linchpin is thankfulness. Why is gratitude so important? True thankfulness is an understanding that we didn't deserve what we received.

We don't use the word thank you this way in the United States. If you work, you may say "Thank you" when your boss hands you your paycheck. After all, it is the polite thing to say. But the truth of our heart in the situation says, *I deserve this.* If your boss decided not to pay you, you would have problems.

Imagine you were hospitalized with a sickness and your friends and your church decided to cover the cost of the bills for thousands of dollars. What would you say? "THANK YOU!!" In fact, you would feel that was far too inadequate a response for such a gesture. You would feel overcome with emotion, and maybe feel undeserving. Two checks: an earned paycheck and an unearned gift. Two different situations. Same two words. And two *completely* different hearts. Wild, unabashed gratitude only comes when we realize that we and our actions had nothing to do with the outcome.

When I was in 8th grade, I was interviewed by the principal of a Christian school as part of pre-enrollment procedures. The principal asked me a question that shifted my heart for the rest of my life. He said, "Why should you be allowed into heaven?" I had never been asked such a thing. I'd just assumed I would be going! "Well, ummm. I am a pretty good kid. My dad is a pastor. I have gone to church my whole life. I have done mostly good things in my life..." My voice trailed off because I knew I didn't know how to answer the question. The principal kindly reminded me that we are saved because of Jesus' actions on the cross, not by our own actions. "Duh!" I thought. I've heard this my whole life, yet my heart operated on the truth that my salvation *did* have something to do with me.

So many of us know that Jesus died for our sins and that we receive the gift of salvation by grace, but that knowledge doesn't always seep into our hearts. If we really were to examine ourselves, we might realize the beliefs in our hearts and the knowledge in our minds are not as congruent as we think. Our burnout problem, therefore, is not due to a lack of information, rather, it is a lack of that information transforming the beliefs in our hearts. We need the things we know to be true about God to actually become core convictions, not just cliches.

Some have said that the distance between heaven and hell is the distance between your head and your heart. We know in our minds that God is everywhere, but we don't believe in our hearts that God is always with us. The most freeing step to experience God's presence is to realize that God doesn't show up based on our actions, He shows up because He wants to. We cannot usher in the presence of God. He is with us. All we need to do is say, *thank you.*

So, does this mean that reading the Bible, praying, spending time in solitude, fasting, worshiping in church with fellow believers means nothing to God? Far from it. I like to think of these acts as invitations to God. When you get an invitation to a wedding, are you now forced to go to that wedding? Or do you decide to attend and show up with a blender by your own free will? God is not a reluctant wedding guest. He is never in debt to our actions. We don't whisper a special prayer to make Him show up.

Instead, when we allocate time, reflection, or action to Him, we are extending an invitation. He is not forced to show up because of our actions. But because of God's great love, He dwells with us. A dangerous place that I have been in and have seen others get into is when we feel that our actions directly correspond to God "showing up." Let me ask you this: if I do something to "make God show up," who is the one in charge? We must never believe that our actions make God show up because that itself makes us bigger than Him. Whenever God's presence feels tangible, we mustn't wonder what we did to make that happen. *Just say thank you!*

At one point in my life, I made a commitment to God. A covenant with Him that I was going to take a 40-day period and spend two uninterrupted hours with Him each day. At first, it was tiring, but then it quickly became so powerful. It felt like I actually began to have a real relationship with God. He was showing me things for people and myself and it was incredible to feel His presence every morning. After that 40-day period, I was fired up so I decided to spend the next 40-days reading the entire Bible. I read from front to back in those days which required a few hours of reading a day. After that, I read the book of John every day for another 30 days. Yes, the whole book. I was on fire for God, and boy was God showing Himself to be real! I began to think to myself that I had finally figured out the formula for making God show up in my life. You can guess what happened next...

All of a sudden: nothing. I couldn't figure it out. God was speaking so clearly and I was doing all the right things, so how could He just disappear like that? The hours I spent with God that were so easy now became difficult. "What is wrong with me?" I thought. "Did I sin?" "Oh no, God must be mad at me." I cried out to God to forgive me for whatever I did and to speak to me again. After a week or two, I was running at the YMCA and God's presence became tangible again! Not on my time, but on His time. I finally felt like I was good again, that I deserved to have God show up in my life. You want to know what God said to me that day? Here it is: "For the last few months, you have done everything right. You spent time with me in the darkness of night. You read my Word. You shared my name with others. I showed up powerfully in your life. Now, I want you to do nothing. And I am going to show up just the same because I want you to know that none of this has anything to do with you." It was stern and kind at the same time. Here I was thinking I was being God's perfect human and in reality, the last 110 days of perfect religion turned out to be a lesson in humility.

I still read the Bible, pray, fast, preach, serve, worship, etc. but I do these things now from a heart posture in gratitude rather than religion. I still struggle with the idea that my actions summon God. I am a recovering Pharisee becoming more like Jesus each day. God is bigger than you and me, and by His grace and the promise of Jesus, He is with us all.

THE VOICE OF GOD

Now that we understand God is with us, we must all recognize that He talks. God isn't awkward. God isn't weird. He doesn't exist in omnipresence just to stare at us in invisibility. God *talks*. Most importantly, He wants to talk to you. And chances are, He already has.

When I was entering my junior year of college, I volunteered as a counselor for a week of high school camp with my local church. This wasn't my Plan A, I'll admit. I wasn't even supposed to be home this particular summer. I was supposed to be playing collegiate summer baseball preparing for a life as a professional baseball player. But an injury sidelined my summer and now I had nothing better to do than bear witness to campfire songs and mosquito bites.

This particular week of camp, the main speaker was teaching about the Holy Spirit. Now, I know I'd been taught about the Holy Spirit before, but for some reason, this week, it finally hit my heart. It *landed*. I was rocked. During the middle of the week, I found myself just outside the snack shack talking with the main speaker when he looked at me and said, "Caleb, what do you want?" I didn't really know the context of this question. I could have said Skittles or a million dollars, but instead, I quickly blurted, "People say, 'God told me...' or 'God said...' I've even heard you say it in your sermons. And I have been in a lot of church services, but have never had God speak to me. I want to hear God's voice."

I had no hope for this pastor to be able to answer that desire. I figured he would do what everyone else did and just offer a cliché to make everything seem better. But his reaction was quite the opposite. He laughed. Then he said, "Want to practice right now?"

Right here? I thought. I had always assumed if God was going to speak, the moment would have to be perfect. Like, there would be a swelling encore and a piano solo, probably "Oceans" by Hillsong UNITED. "Sure," I responded skeptically.

He told me that God desires to talk to us and that He wanted to talk to me. He placed a hand on my shoulder and then asked the Holy Spirit to bring a word to my mind of something that He loved about me. After all, if God loves all of us, certainly He would have one characteristic that He loves about me. So, I mustered with all my might the desire and will power to make God talk to me. But no word came. *Nothing*. The pastor then encouraged me that there was nothing wrong with me and that I didn't have to try to *make* God talk to me. He can speak under His own power. I don't need to do anything to make God talk to me; He just will. All I need to do is listen. But not necessarily with my ears.

The pastor told me to look in my mind for a word to pop up, and to just say that word out loud. We prayed again, and sure enough, I saw a word pop into my head immediately: *laughter*.

Laughter? Did God love my laugh? I was still a little uncertain because surely it couldn't be that ordinary to hear the voice of God, right? So, we practiced again. This time, we asked the Holy Spirit to show me something that He loved about the pastor leading me through this exercise. A word came swiftly: *justice*. That wasn't a word I threw around a lot; I knew it wasn't one that would come to me that fast. But that word encouraged the pastor; it meant something to him.

In that simple exchange, the voice of God became abundant. I could now have a true relationship with the God I had given my life to. I realized that God had actually been speaking to me many times in the past and I didn't even realize it. I just called it my conscience, but it was God. God was always near me and speaking to me. And in that moment, I finally learned how to hear it.

The following day, God spoke that He wanted to heal me of my concussion by having my youth pastor pray for me. I never had a symptom again. That concussion was the whole reason I was at the camp in the first place. It always astounds me how God uses all things for His good.

I don't expect my story to be your story, but I do expect and know that God speaks to you. We just need to get tuned in. To listen, to hear, to communicate. Communication is a huge part of being in love with Him. Being in love with someone that never communicates with you sounds more like a celebrity crush than the relationship God wants to have with us.

There are three main ways God communicates with us: (1) the Bible, (2) through people, and (3) directly to us. We covered the importance of the Word of God in Chapter 3, so I hope you are still being washed by the word daily. The Bible is so essential to understanding God's heart, and it becomes even more alive when the Holy Spirit speaks to us about the scriptures He inspired. It also doesn't take much effort to realize that people speak out God's voice. In fact, that is my prayer for this very book: that God will use my voice as His own. But I don't want to just depend on the Bible and others. I want God to communicate with me directly. For those of us who have ever mulled over a massive question or change in our life, we can take heart: God will actually show us Himself and His plans for us by communicating directly with us.

As we first start out, we will notice that these three communication areas are like distinct silos that we work on independently. However, as we keep learning and practicing hearing God's voice, we will begin to notice that the three areas work together and even start to blend into the realization that there is no place we can turn that God *isn't* speaking to us. I love when God gives me a thought that aligns with scripture, which is then the focus of the Sunday sermon. When that happens to me, I say, "Loud and clear, God."

I urge us all that The Rejuvenated Life actively has all three of these communicative methods working at all times: His living

Word, the words of others, and His words to us. It's the voice of God tripod. If we take away one of the legs, everything falls over. If we get too heavily dependent on one area, we will become off balance. We need all three working to truthfully understand what God has for us today.

In my life, I have noticed that the more I read the Bible, the more I can understand His voice when directed toward me. I also know that the more I am around others who hear from God, the more I hear from God. Learning to discern God's voice is a progression. It takes time. Jesus described all things Kingdom like a mustard seed. It starts small, but grows to be big. Don't be in a rush to accomplish this skill, for God's voice cannot be achieved, it can only be heard. Take the time and just practice discerning it every day.

A common phrase that Jesus would say after a teaching is "He who has ears to hear, let him hear." Essentially, Jesus is making a distinction that just because you hear physically doesn't mean you hear spiritually. God doesn't value hearing with our ears. He values hearing with our spirits. In our world, words are simply used to convey ideas so that people can have the same thoughts at the same time. But God doesn't need words because he can communicate directly into our spirits. This is where phrases like "I don't know how I know; I just know!" come from. This is how we get a gut feeling to reach out to encourage a friend right when he or she needs it most. It's not a mere coincidence. It's a method of communication.

In his book *Imagine Heaven,* John Burke notes that a segment of people who had near death experiences and saw visions of heaven said that communication in heaven wasn't with words, but rather was communication directly from spirit to spirit.[7] This type of communication completely eliminates misunderstanding because I know we have each had times where our words failed to adequately communicate what we felt, or our words were misunderstood because of how someone else felt. Spirit to spirit communication involves more than just the communication of ideas, but also the communication of the feelings associated with those ideas.

I know that God can do and speak however He wants to. There is no one way that God speaks. But I find that spirit communication is the one many of us struggle with the most. Reading our Bible and seeking Godly advice feels far more productive and measurable than a mysteriously and often inaudible exchange with God. So let me simplify a bit.

Have you ever talked to yourself? That's the realm I am talking about. This is the realm in which you hear your voice, God's voice, and in reality, a lot of demonic voices as well. Most of the time we claim all of these voices under one big umbrella and call it our conscience. That is far from the truth. Our inner life boasts not one, but many voices, and to hear from God with utmost clarity, we must begin the process of distinguishing whose voice is whose.

In Psalm 29:3-9, the voice of God is described in a few different ways. "The voice of the Lord is over the waters; The voice of the Lord is powerful; the voice of the Lord is majestic. The voice of the Lord breaks the cedars; The voice of the Lord strikes with flashes of lightning. The voice of the Lord shakes the desert; The voice of the Lord twists the oaks" (NIV). Essentially, there are no limits to the voice of God. It is big and powerful.

But when we zoom in to focus on the last two verses of this psalm, we find some key characteristics of the voice of the Lord that will help us to distinguish His voice from others: "The Lord sits enthroned over the flood; the Lord is enthroned as King forever. The Lord gives strength to his people; the Lord blesses his people with peace" (Psalm 29:10-11, NIV).

First, "The Lord sits enthroned over the flood." The voice of the Lord is bigger than our problems. If we ever experience a voice in our heads that is intimidated by our problems or in fear of troubles, this is not the voice of God. The Lord is over the flood, not in it. He is bigger than our life and anything involving our life. He is not thrown off by any decision or situation. If the voice inside you is shaky, it's not God. He is not threatened by any situation because He is over it all.

Second, "the Lord is enthroned as King forever." The voice of God always proclaims Jesus as Lord. In my experience with demonic voices, the quickest way to tell whether someone is experiencing demonic voices is to ask them to proclaim Jesus is Lord. Two things happen. Either they won't say it, or they do say it and immediately, the voices begin to subside. A few weeks ago, I did this with a college student. He told me that when we started talking, his mind was like rough seas. After we talked and he proclaimed Jesus as Lord, he said he never experienced such peace and that his thoughts were like a placid pond. Praise God! There is only one Lord and it is Jesus Christ. The voice of God will always acknowledge Jesus as Lord.

Third, "The Lord gives strength to his people." If the voices in our head leave us feeling like we are in a fog or mentally drained, this is not God. The voice of God is specific and gives strength. Even when God is reprimanding us, He will give us the strength to respond. Pastor Gregg Paris once said, "I have said a lot of things to God, but it's the things God has said to me that changed my life." When He speaks, He strengthens.

Finally, "the Lord blesses his people with peace." If we do not experience peace, it isn't God's voice. Jesus is called the Prince of Peace. There is no peace outside of Jesus. Whether the Father, Jesus or the Holy Spirit is speaking to you, you will experience peace. Even if God is not pleased with the life you are living, there will be a level of grace around His voice. God has disciplined me and I can tell you this; I have never experienced anything kinder in the world than the discipline of God. There is abundant peace with His voice.

It's important, though, for us to wisely discern the difference between God's unshakeable peace and our life's temporary moments of peace. Let's say that a person is praying and seeking wise counsel as they decide which of two job opportunities they should pursue. They wrestle for weeks with decision fatigue, and the process of deciding is so exhausting that, as soon as they do decide, they feel an immediate weight off their shoulders. Is this the peace of God, or is it the relief of a decision finally made? Conversely, let's say they finally make a decision and, suddenly, they feel sick inside. Is this the unrest of God, or is it the doubt of a decision?

To know, we must give time. Don't always trust the initial feelings after a big decision. If possible, wait 24-48 hours to let the dust settle on a decision and then we can better gauge whether we are experiencing God given peace or God given unrest. A practice that I have come to find greatly helpful when dealing with big decisions is to make a decision in my heart before proclaiming it to a bunch of other people. This allows me to live with it for a day or two to make sure I am at true peace. Simply coming to a big life decision and 15 minutes later making a Facebook announcement is not the way of wisdom. Allowing time gives us the ability to wade through the initial emotions of a conclusion while still giving the opportunity to reverse course if we do recognize that we have gone astray.

The more we are in real communication with God, the more peace will flow through our lives. You and I don't have to ask if someone hears from God; their lives will show it. If you are someone that has a lot of anxiety and worry, I would love to invite you to acknowledge the presence of God and hear His voice. I love the lyrics from the hymn *In the Garden.*

> And he walks with me and he talks with me
> And he tells me I am his own
> And the joy we share as we tarry there
> None other has ever known

What a joy it is to know that the God of the universe desires to walk with us and talk with us. I pray that we would reciprocate even a portion of the joy God has walking and talking with us as we walk and talk with Him. So, let's get going. Sit down. Be Still. Don't try. Just listen.

THE REJUVENATION PROJECT

Want to practice hearing God's voice? Pause and ask the Holy Spirit to speak to you. I like to start by asking the Holy Spirit because His voice is probably one we are more familiar with than we realize because He lives in all believers. Then, pull out a notebook and get two different colored pens - one for God and one for you - and write down a question. Any question you have for God.

A great question to start with is "What do you love about me?" The next step is to pause and listen with your spirit, not your ears. You may see or hear pictures, a word, a phrase, a song, a color, a memory, a vision, etc. Write down what comes to mind. Don't analyze it before you write it down. Just write it. Afterwards, you can process.

To process the answer to the question of "What does God love about me?", I'd start by asking yourself, "Is that true?" Often, it's not just true, but the very core attribute about you. Oftentimes, I come back to a notebook of conversations years later and I can see more clearly whether something was from God or if it was just my ideas. Most of the time it is God's voice though. You will not be perfect. It's okay to mess up. The key is that you start.

Once I get more comfortable with the process, I may ask the Holy Spirit to show me something that He loves about my wife or someone close to me. I would take whatever I hear or see and tell it to my wife. I wouldn't start by saying, "Hey honey, God says you are a beautiful singer." I would say, "Hey honey, I really enjoy when you sing." I would then wait to see her response. Since I know that God loves it about her, I know my compliment should strike a stronger chord in her if it was from God. If it was just my idea, it will still be nice, but may not be as moving.

The key when practicing is to not initially attest what you say to be from God. The best thing you can do is to say it was from you. If it seems to move someone, then you need to give credit that God told you. If it ends up just being something you made up, then you do not want to make God sound like He doesn't know what He is talking about. The only true way to know if something is from

God is if it comes true. If it didn't happen like "God said," then it wasn't Him. If hindsight is 20/20, it also applies to recognizing God's voice. At some point, you are going to have to act on what you believe God is saying to find out if it's true. (More on that in the next chapter.)

I also want to encourage you to find other people that you believe hear from God. Begin to ask them questions and learn as much as you can. Sometimes I run ideas that I think might be God's voice by other people. I will tell them what I think God is telling me. I will ask them if that sounds consistent with God's ways. They will affirm or offer a correction using the scriptures or their prior experiences. This step is helpful to build confidence in hearing God. Just like any friend, the more time you spend with them, the more you pick up on their tendencies. God is no different. Always remember that God's voice to us will never contradict what is said in scripture. Now get listening!

CHAPTER SIX

OBEDIENCE

"THERE IS A WAY that appears to be right, but in the end it leads to death" (Proverbs 14:12, NIV). This is one of the most disheartening verses in all of scripture to me. How are we to know what to do if we can't even trust our own insights that appear to be correct? My life *feels* right, but what if I'm just walking toward the same death that every other "right" person has experienced? I want my last days to be my best days. I want to finish strong. I want to run my race well. If I leave this up to my intuition, I can only predict a future of deception and burnout. Thankfully, we've been given more than mere intuition. We've been given a principle that ensures we will live the life we are truly called to live. Simply put, that principle is obedience.

Obedience is probably one of the first principles we learned growing up. Maybe this is why many of us detest it so much. From our first memories, we are told what to do and when to do it by people who may or may not even follow their own advice. Ever the rebels, we kids would dream of the day we received our driver's license, moved out, or turned 21 so we could finally be our own boss. We spend our whole lives aspiring to do what we want to do when we want to do it, but in reality, that aspiration is the very thing that leads to death. To truly get the rejuvenated life we desire, we must not seek our own desires, but rather seek to have a heart that submits to the desires of our God.

We cannot be in charge if we wish to enter the Kingdom of Heaven. Jesus said, "Truly I tell you, unless you change and become like little children, you will never enter the kingdom of heaven" (Matthew 18:3, NIV). There are a lot of truths about little children, but one we all understand is that it's not good for little kids to be in charge. There is no small child that can properly navigate life and all its needs on their own. This is why every child should have guidance from adults.

Similarly, we are in the infancy of eternity and should not expect that we know enough to navigate the Kingdom of Heaven without guidance. Therefore, God can only give us the life He destined for us if we trust Him with our life and let Him guide it. At first, it may seem like this level of obedience is meant to take away all our fun, but in reality, God wants to give us all His glory. The truth of Proverbs 14:12, inverted, reads like this: "There is a way that appears to be wrong, but in the end, it leads to life." Why? Because it only *appears* to be wrong. We, as humans, tend to take our thoughts, opinions, actions, and will and make them secondary to the thoughts, opinions, actions, and will of God. We must give precedence to God's opinion before our own opinion.

If our life is God-ordained, it will require that we do things that we don't want to do, or that seem foolish to the rest of the world. The ultimate way to know whether or not we trust God with our life is to watch our response when we sense God leading us to do something we don't necessarily want to do. If we shy away from the tough, hard things that God asks us to do, then we should question whether we truly trust God. Now, if you don't have a gut reaction to shy away from the tough, hard things that God asks you to do, then maybe you are a psychopath. (Kidding.) But truthfully, I have never met anyone that liked obedience. It feels better to be in charge! It's more comfortable. But comfort now does not bring comfort tomorrow.

Once we are truly submitted to Him, God graciously breaks us of our comforts so He can be our comfort. But, there's an important distinction to make here. It is *God's* job to stretch our comfort zones, not ours. If we take it upon ourselves to bring on the hard times, then we will rob ourselves and our families of godly blessings. We will cause our lives to be harder than perhaps they were intended to be. The Rejuvenated Life lives within God's will for our life. God has a purpose for our life, and we want to live a majority of our days smack dab in the middle of that purpose.

We have all heard it said, "God will never give you more than you can handle." And sure, I can get behind that statement. Usually, we like to throw around this adage when somebody is going through a tough time in their life. But sometimes, I admittedly wonder: "Are you sure God gave you this tough time?" Is God behind the trouble or blessing we are going through? Is it a tough time because God is molding us, or are we simply reaping the harvest of previous disobedience whether it was intentional disobedience or not?

We need to be tuned in to what God is actually doing in our lives. If we are being blessed and it wasn't from God, let's not be so happy. If we are in trouble, but God has us there, we must rejoice. This begs the question, "How do we know if God is behind our trouble or blessing? I wish I could know definitively, but the best and only answer I know is *time*. The plans of God are revealed over time, not in a moment. I have been proven a fool many times for claiming something was or wasn't from God before truly seeing the bigger picture later on in life. Therefore, the best way to understand our current situations in regards to God's guidance is to look at the past.

When my dad gives marriage advice, he says, "Your marriage today will be the product of what you did 6 months ago." Similarly, if we want to understand the fruit of today, let's look at what we did 6-12 months earlier. Let's say, for example, someone started a business and it's now booming. They're now filthy rich. Is this God blessing them? It depends. To know, they must think back to what they did 6-12 months earlier. Did they get to the boom because they worked harder, or was it because God gifted them with an innovative idea or they met the right person at the right time? A boom in business due to one's own efforts alone will rarely prove to be a blessing in the end. After all, there is no shortage of business owners succeeding at the expense of another area of their lives: health, family, relationships. On the other hand, if the business owner had an inclination from God and obeyed it boldly, I would imagine they will be blessed continually - in more areas than just the business at hand.

This axiom leads to another principle about obedience to God: obedience *leaks*. If God asks us to do something in our marriage, those actions will bless our family and work life, too. In fact, there is no area of our life that obedience to God will *not* bless. Now, if obedience leaks, then control *steals*. If we work by our own efforts and control, we will bless an area of our life at the expense of another. God can create from nothing; His blessings are endless. We cannot create from nothing, so if we live by our own efforts, we have to expense blessings from other areas. This is why many successful people in business lack blessing in their home; their business boomed at the cost of their family. We could all name examples of many situations in which growth in one area required sacrifice in another: health, marriage, work, hobbies, friendships. But there is no area of life that is off limits to the abundant plans of God. In the Kingdom of God, growth is multiplied, not divided.

Our harvest today is largely due to our obedience from the past. This is not just obedience to the Word of God, but also to the natural laws He established. Though there are no Bible verses against eating junk food, we know inherently that empty calories are not what our bodies require to sustain life. If we were to consistently walk in forgiveness and were daily washed by the Word, but we never once ate a vegetable, we would still fall short of The Rejuvenated Life because our physical bodies wouldn't function well enough to live out what God intended for us.

The truth is this: many of our belief systems are rooted in Greek philosophy, which often tries to separate body, mind, and spirit. But the cultural lens of the ancient Greeks doesn't fit the ways of God. God doesn't separate these entities, and instead, calls us to love Him the same in all areas, not just the spiritual ones (Matthew 22:37). God's definition of blessing and trouble are not the same as the world's. Such is the quest of following God. Let's not simply rely on our intuition to decide if we're living well. We must remember the Proverbs 14:12 principle, trusting God and looking honestly at our life - past and present - to know which way is truly right.

TO OBEY IS TO LOVE

Now that we have established the necessity of obedience, how do we know *what* to obey? This is where we rely on our growth from earlier chapters. We know He speaks to us through the Bible, directly to our spirits, through people and any other way He deems. We know that, in time, we will continue to grow better at distinguishing His voice.

But just because we hear God doesn't mean we obey God. Obedience is the separator. It's time we start valuing doing what God says to do, not just hearing Him. When it comes to obedience, there is no other scripture that sets a stronger tone than when Jesus says in John 14:23-24:

> "Anyone who loves me will obey my teaching. My Father will love them, and we will come to them and make our home with them. Anyone who does not love me will not obey my teaching. These words you hear are not my own; they belong to the Father who sent me." (NIV)

If I were to ask you if Jesus loves you, you would probably say "Of Course!" You would be correct. If I were to ask you if you love Jesus, you may also have a similar answer. But would you be correct? We don't have to guess. There is only one measure of our love for Jesus and that is our obedience to Him.

To be clear, while obedience is action-oriented, salvation is not. To be saved, we do not have to do anything other than confess that Jesus is Lord and believe that He rose from the dead (Romans 10:9-10). There isn't a resume required for salvation; it's by grace we have been saved. But obedience is what comes next. It's the living, breathing evidence of a decision to love Christ.

If you ever heard a salvation invitation at a church, the phrase commonly used is "Will you give your life to Jesus?" When we say yes to that question, who now has our life? Jesus. I hate to sound obvious, but even I forget this principle. If we gave our life to Jesus, this means that we no longer have the rights to our life and our decisions. We handed them over to Jesus to be Lord of our life. Salvation is a great gift, but we must truly give our life to Him. We cannot receive salvation and remain in charge of our life. Salvation and control are not compatible.

> Not everyone who says to me, 'Lord, Lord,' will enter the kingdom of heaven, *but only the one who does the will of my Father who is in heaven.* Many will say to me on that day, 'Lord, Lord, did we not prophesy in your name and in your name drive out demons and in your name perform many miracles?' Then I will tell them plainly, 'I never knew you. Away from me, you evildoers!' (Matthew 7:21-23, NIV)

There are people who will claim Jesus as Lord that do not enter the Kingdom of Heaven. The people who do enter are the ones who do the will of the Father. Our greatest assurance that we are in the Kingdom is to look at our life and figure out the times we have done something because God asked us to do it. Even if it was inconvenient. Even if it felt foolish. Even if it didn't make any sense at the time, or still doesn't. If we can look at the times we followed the will of God over our own desires, we are walking in love with Jesus.

Just think. God is not interested in us saying a one-time prayer. He is interested in us denying our own will to follow His every day! I don't want to be married to a wife that showed up on a wedding day, but was never considerate of me ever again. We know that doesn't make for a healthy marital relationship, so why would we assume it would make for a healthy spiritual one? Love is a choice that requires action. Not our desired actions, but the actions God desires for us. This is why it is so important to read the Bible, listen to the Holy Spirit, and be around other people that listen to God. By doing these things, we can truly discover God's desires for us.

Here is how we can practically walk out obedience. Whenever we read, feel, or think about doing something that might be from the Lord, we should ask this one question: "If I do what I just read, felt or thought, what will it cost me or others?" If the answer is nothing or very minimal, just do it! No more questions or prayer really needs to happen. There is a high chance it is God leading our path. If we feel the urge to give to the homeless person, just give it! If we need to pray for someone, just do it. Most of the obedience God is going to ask of us might only be possible within a 10-second window. We have to take action or else we miss it.

If we feel prompted to do something that will cost us or others something more significant, we must submit this to further prayer and counsel from others. This process shouldn't involve many years though. If we feel the obedience God is asking of us is a little weightier, we probably have more time to process, but not an endless amount of time.

For instance, imagine God asked you to quit your job to homeschool your kids. This is a weightier decision than paying for the groceries of the person ahead of you at the grocery store. One decision requires immediate action, the other should require some planning and processing. If you spent 3 years wondering if you should homeschool your kids, your child may actually graduate before you obey. This would be disobedience. In the period of prayer and discernment, a small part of the process is "Should I do this?" and a lot more of the time is spent on "Okay God, how do I do this?" Prayer, fasting, and counsel are greatly helpful when walking in these calls to obedience. God regularly asks people to do things that are hard. Simply, thinking something is impossible doesn't mean He didn't still ask you to do it.

Now, I want to address something important here. The voice of God does not always, or often, lead to a tidy, sterile, perfect situation. Remember the many descriptors we discovered for the voice of God in Chapter 5? The voice of the Lord breaks the cedars; The voice of the Lord strikes with flashes of lightning. The voice of the Lord shakes the desert; The voice of the Lord twists the oaks (Psalm 29). That doesn't sound very tidy, does it?

Sometimes the thing God is asking us to do will be hard and painful. It will feel like we are betraying someone, uprooting our own life, or even causing hurt to someone else's life. If there are consequences to where you sense God could be leading you, truly take some time to pray, fast, and talk to mentors in your life. We have all heard of instances where misled and confused zealots have killed their whole family because "God told them to." This is a clear and extreme example. It wouldn't take long for an outside mentor to see that murder is *not* the voice of God.

While we can't rely on others to listen to God *for* us, we can still ask opinions of those who regularly hear His voice. But we mustn't ask the opinion of those who do not care about God or are not following His ways. Remember, there is a way that *seems* right... God will regularly ask us to do things that contradict what we think is right, so seek wise mentors that model a life surrendered to Jesus.

I'd encourage us all to live our life with the assumption that God never stops talking to us. This means obedience can come at any moment. I know for me that when God asks me to do something, my first reaction is to think why that isn't a good idea. When temptation comes though, I seem not to hesitate in action. Obedience gives 20/20 vision. We will never truly know if it was the voice of God unless we obey. The more we obey, the more we will become confident in His guidance as He directs our path, whisper by whisper.

Obedience is what deepens that gentle whisper into a rumbling roar. Without obedience, it can become nearly impossible to raise the volume loud enough to hear God's quiet presence. The truth is, there are many voices in our head, and at any given moment, we are either hearing from God, ourselves, or a demon. We need to recognize which is which.

Some people think we need to obey when we know 100% that

God was asking us to do it. But from my experiences and the others who have walked with God longer than I, very rarely do we hear the voice of God with no doubt attached. If God is moving, the devil won't be too far away casting doubt and lies. This is not to say that when you obey there are endless doubts that arise, but I do recognize in those early moments of an instruction from God, there will be a fight to keep us from obeying. If we feel prompted to do something risky and there is no doubt involved or we believe we are the exception, maybe we should question if God is the one leading that effort. We shouldn't be cast aside by some resistance when God leads us. Typically, we should be more concerned if there is no resistance so that we make sure we are not walking by the way that appears to be right, but in the end leads to death.

If we are 25% certain that God is speaking and the thing He is asking won't hurt others, just do it! We may be surprised. We will be right sometimes and we may be wrong sometimes. It is a better testimony to share before Jesus someday that even if we missed it, we were seeking to learn, hear and most importantly *obey* His voice. I even wonder if sometimes we do get His voice mistaken as our own, but if we do it unto Him, He will still be honored. We need not just hear His voice. We need to take action!

In the parable of the ten bags of Gold, Jesus describes the Kingdom of Heaven like a master who entrusted differing amounts of gold to three servants. He gave one servant 10 bags of gold. Another 5 bags. And still another 1 bag. The first two invested their gold, but the last buried it in the ground. The master commended the two servants that took the bags of gold they were given and invested them, but he scorned the one who did nothing with his bag (Matthew 25:14-30). The voice of God is gold. Don't bury it. Don't ignore it. Obey it!

Obedience took center stage in my life in January of 2020. I was listening to a sermon about how to make 2020 the best year of your life. You know, the classic New Year sermon that every pastor preaches. However, this pastor made it crystal clear: "If you want the best day, best month, best year, best life, there is only one thing to do... make Jesus your Lord."

We have heard this sentiment spoken many times after, say, an athlete wins the Super Bowl or World Series. Elated and exhausted, they'll hold their trophy high and proclaim, "I'd like to first thank my Lord and Savior Jesus Christ." But there is a difference between a Lord and a Savior.

Let's be honest; many of us are pretty comfortable with the idea of Jesus as our Savior. We know we sin, but praise Jesus for taking our punishment! We are less comfortable with a Lord. Having a Lord means we have no choice. We have given up our independence. We are completely at the mercy of our Lord. When we use the phrase "lord it over," we mean someone or something that asserts absolute dominance and has the right to do so. If Jesus is truly our Lord, then we have no rights except whatever He deems.

I was convicted after that service, because I knew Jesus saved me, but He wasn't completely my Lord. I liked being saved and going to heaven, but still wanted to make my own decisions in life. Naturally, this is not the recipe for a dynamic Christian life. So once I got home, I prayed a dangerous prayer: "Holy Spirit, teach me how to make Jesus the Lord of my life."

I sat on my couch, still and quiet. Immediately, the thought came to my conscience: *Delete your to-do list.*

Now, I have always been a planner. I remember making to-do lists as early as 6th grade, setting a goal of what I needed to do and then completing it. It was satisfying to have the feeling of accomplishment. For years, I would deem a day good or bad based on whether I got everything on my list checked off that day. I won many awards and scholarships in high school and college for my disciplined, task-oriented lifestyle. People aspired to structure their days like I could - check, check, check! But you know what? God wasn't as impressed.

I knew that if I wanted to grow closer to God, then I needed to move to the next level with Him. I had been orchestrating my steps, but God wanted to be in charge. And so, in what felt like an overwhelming task of obedience, I hit "Delete" on the document from my computer and phone.

For the ensuing weeks, I felt directionless and unproductive, but now I look back on my life and see that as one of the most productive things I ever did. Most of the God ordained plans He had for me in the future would have never made it into my checklist. Chance encounters with people. Out-of-the-blue gifts. Creative ideas. None of it would have come by my doing. You know why? Because I am not God. When I stopped controlling my steps, God brought me to a greater life. I make a bad Lord. I want Jesus to be my Lord.

A few months later, another thought came to my head: *Get rid of your TV.* As with everything God has asked me to do, I immediately reasoned why that was a bad idea. "That thought can't be from God." I said to myself. "I have a brand-new baby girl that is up all night. We are entering the deep dark winter in Indiana, and there is a pandemic that makes us stay at home. The TV is keeping us sane." I considered the idea to be my own and not God's, but the thought never left my mind. I felt pressure and even sick to my stomach to obey, but the TV was a step too much for me at the time. I wrestled with it for weeks, but then moved on.

But then, I heard it again. As I was praying one night, the thought returned: *Get rid of the TV*. Once more, I wrestled. This felt like something I just couldn't obey, or didn't need to. Finally, peace came over me as I heard in my spirit, "Okay, don't worry about it. You can keep your TV."

"Thank you God for understanding," I thought. I made it out scratch free and I was living in the grace of God - no longer tormented by the TV. What I didn't realize at the time is that God is not in debt to me. He doesn't need me to do anything for Him. He is not on my clock, nor my payroll. If I don't obey, He moves on to someone that will do what He says. He did it graciously and lovingly, but I didn't obey and He was done waiting. There wasn't any condemnation whatsoever from Him. In fact, I truly felt like I convinced God my way was better. Thankfully, He gave me another chance later on.

Three or four months would pass before I would wake up one Monday morning with a song stuck in my head. The day before at church, my pastor preached on music and how God often puts a song in our heart for us to worship Him with. I was amazed that God was truly calling me to worship with a song. I had the tune to the song and the first line of lyrics going through my head, but couldn't remember anything more to be able to Google the song to find it. In fact, I hadn't even heard the song in *years*. This particular song was used as the alarm clock for a week of camp I attended over 5 years earlier. Groggy and sunburnt, a cabinful of teens would wake up to a few chords and that first line before my friend Jeremy would shut it off and we'd hit the showers. But that song - that line - was stuck on loop, and I couldn't shake it.

I finally texted my friend at 10pm that night: "Hey Jeremy, I know it has been a while and I hope you are doing well. I have a strange request; do you remember your alarm clock song that you had at camp 5 years ago?" He responded, "Hey man, I have only had three songs as my alarm over the last 10 years so it will be one of these... Do you have time to talk for a minute?"

He called and told me what God was doing in his life and encouraged me to listen to a sermon called "Ascend the Mountain" by Chad Norris. I thanked him and hung up, then searched for the song. But as soon as I listened to the song, the whole worshipful feeling I had all day and tune of the song left me. I went from feeling like God was leading me in one moment to *absolutely nothing* in the next. I was on a hunt for worship and it ended in a dead end.

So, I decided to follow Jeremy's advice and listen to the sermon. Within minutes, my spirit came back to life. The pastor was calling those listening to live in radical obedience to God's desires rather than their own. For 40 minutes, I was completely stirred. As the sermon ended, I pondered the pastor's sermon and asked myself, "How do I live in complete obedience?" Sitting in my living room, I looked up, and there it was: the TV. Clearly, I heard God say in my spirit, "I'll give you another chance. Get rid of your TV." This time, I obeyed.

This is not a new thing God is doing. Even now, I look back and see how the whole day I was not being led to worship through music, but through obedience. "Does the Lord delight in burnt offerings and sacrifices as much as in obeying the Lord? To obey is better than sacrifice, and to heed is better than the fat of rams" (1 Samuel 15:22, NIV). The greatest worship we can give to God is our obedience.

In the context of this verse, God had given specific instructions for Saul to carry out. God wanted Saul to wipe out Israel's enemies *completely*. Saul did that, almost, but decided to leave the best animals alive to be used for sacrifice and worship to God. Saul carried out about 90% of those instructions and felt pretty confident, as you and I probably would. But God was not impressed. In fact, at that moment, God rejected Saul as King.

These are not my words; this is God's heart. If we want to love and worship God, we have to obey. 90% obedience is not obedience. We must completely do what God has asked us to do. When you disobey, please repent as quickly as humanly possible and pray that God does not reject you. You may think that is severe, but the only way to make it to the end of our life without burning out is to do exactly what God says, when he says to do it, without any shortcuts. There is only one way that's right and it is God's way.

God cares about us and our life. This is why He calls us to obedience. I will never truly know what the biggest, most important acts of obedience I have done - or haven't - in my life. Neither will you. There is a bigger picture that only God can see. Obedience acknowledges that God is the bigger, better, and stronger party in the relationship. Obedience says, "Jesus, you are Lord and I am not." Even more so, it says, "Jesus, I love you."

THE REJUVENATION PROJECT

If you are ready, pray a dangerous prayer. "Holy Spirit, how do I make Jesus the Lord of my life?" Just see what comes to mind. I would also ask you to think through your past and ask "Have I been running away from something God has asked me to do?" If so, pray for forgiveness and a second chance. The second chance may not be the same thing though, so don't just go back to His original prompting. Don't assume anything. Ask Him to speak fresh again and be diligent to obey.

After reading a section on obedience, you may start to think that God has an opinion on everything you do. It doesn't appear to be in His nature to micromanage us. When we give Him our life, He doesn't micromanage it, He guides it. If you think God has an opinion on everything you do during a day, you are probably mixing in other voices and your own opinions.

If you are new to this obedience thing, God will probably not ask you to do more than one or two things a day or even over a week or two. He is God though, so it could be more, but I can assure you that if you feel pressure to obey 30 different specific things a day, it's not Him.

Why am I so certain about this? God is not in a rush. He cares more about our character than what we do on the outside. He also doesn't wish to steal our creative ability and choice. God steps in to make sure we are going on the right path, but then gives us freedom to enjoy Him and His creation uniquely. Also, the desire to obey a multitude of things a day seems to fall under the enemy's deceptive strategy called *proving.* When Jesus was tempted in the desert, the devil's strategy with Jesus was to tempt Him to prove His power (Matthew 4). Similarly, the devil likes to take the obedience lesson and say to us "prove it." So, if you feel overwhelmed by the number of things you need to obey, just say, "I don't have to prove anything," and then sit until those overwhelming thoughts subside. Then continue on the journey trusting, listening, and obeying. If you feel overwhelmed by one thing, then it's likely God.

As you work on obedience, at the end of each day, write down what you did that day to obey God. You may also realize that you didn't obey God, but looking back, you wish you did. That is good to understand, but try not to default to hindsight.

As you get stronger at obedience and understanding the heart of God, you may notice that God gives you a word of obedience for a whole season or an undisclosed time period. This might be like "Become a man of my word." "Be a woman who never gossips." "Father your kids before you pour into other kids." The timing of that season usually corresponds to how long it takes you to obey. A specific call to obedience can be for a singular moment, a season, or even a lifetime.

You can't rush past God. If you ever feel like God has stopped talking to you or you feel distant from Him, go back to the scriptures and go back to the last thing He asked you to obey. It's like looking for anything in life: go back to the last place you had it. Chances are, if you feel distant from God, you may not have completely obeyed what God asked you to do previously.

Finally, don't assume God only talks to us if He wants us to do something. If the large percentage of God's words to you are things you need to obey, then you are missing a lot of His voice. A good parent doesn't boss their kid around all day. They spend time with them. They share delight with them. They speak love and joy and peace to them. God will speak with you about how to obey, but He will always speak more about things He loves about you and other random things about your life. Invite Him into those everyday conversations, too.

Decide today to be a person that ceaselessly obeys God. God doesn't rush people through obedience school. He does a thorough job making sure we can be trusted with His plans. This will be a lifelong journey. The longer you live a life of obedience, the more you begin to know God. The more you know God, the less painful obedience feels because you are becoming like God and trusting Him more. When you follow through with what He commands, you can be certain your last days will be your best days living in the life God has for you.

CHAPTER SEVEN

FORGIVENESS

FOR MOST PEOPLE working through The Rejuvenation Project, this is often the chapter that separates the ones that come to find the freedom they have desired and the ones who slip back into their former way of living that leads to burnout. The concepts in this chapter may take the longest to work through, but they will also bring the greatest relief. If you have arrived here by steadily putting into practice the concepts you've learned thus far, well done! As I shared in the introduction of this book, each chapter you read is a building block to The Rejuvenated Life. Skipping over one or rushing through each may cause the whole plan to fall apart.

If you're reading a chapter daily, you've likely not had time to feel much change. But if you've been taking time to work through this book at a slower pace - or better yet, rereading it as you practice in faith, this is where you'll notice The Rejuvenation Project kick into high gear. Buckle up! There may be some turbulence ahead, but trust me, we have to go through a bumpy ride to meet the freedom we were made to live in.

In this chapter, we're exploring forgiveness. This word brings up a variety of emotions for us. Each of us has different reasons to forgive or be forgiven. The level of hurt that we experience is different, but remember: this isn't a competition between who has the least or most hurt. Pain hurts for all. Pain is relative. So many of us don't receive freedom from the pain of our past because we waste time comparing our pain to the pain of someone else's past. And so, to begin, we have to address our *own* pain.

It is difficult to surmise all the ways that a person could be hurt, yet it's not difficult to guess the source of them: *people.* Organizations can't hurt people. Jobs can't hurt people. The government can't hurt people. It may feel like these systems can hurt people, but let's think, who is behind each of these systems? People. People hurt people. We may know the people or we may not with larger areas of injustice, but we must all acknowledge there is another living, breathing soul associated with any bitterness we feel.

When we are talking about pain, it is important to recognize there is a person on the other side of your pain. That person may even be you. The pain caused by the wrongdoer may not, and most often, isn't intentional, but it is pain nonetheless. Intentions can never be judged accurately on earth by any human, and so we do not consider them in the process of forgiveness. In fact, not only do we not consider the intentions behind our pain, but the person who hurt us isn't even involved in the process of forgiveness. Even if the pain you feel was caused by someone else, the keys to freedom, healing, and forgiveness are not held in *their* hands. These keys are held in *yours*.

Have you ever heard the folklore of how natives from all over the world learned to capture monkeys? The story goes like this: a coconut or gourd is found and hollowed-out through a small hole. The hunter puts some delicious food in the coconut and waits. In time, a monkey approaches the trap and attempts to eat the food inside. But while the hole is large enough for the monkey to get his hand in, as soon as he makes a fist to grab the food, his hand is now too large to squeeze it out. The truth is this: the monkey could be free at any time, but he must unclench his fist and let go. But choosing *not* to let go will be the very thing that causes danger to his life.

Unforgiveness is a monkey's trap. It's not that we are trapped and someone else is holding us hostage. We are in a trap and we hold the keys at the same time. At any point, we can be free *if we want to be.*

Before we go any further in The Rejuvenation Project, we have to choose today to forgive. Forgiveness is not a feeling. It is a choice. Forgiveness doesn't happen unless it is chosen. Even today, there may be hurts that we thought we had worked through, but we still carry deep wounds. No matter how painful those wounds are, we can choose today to open our fist and let go so we can be free.

Letting go doesn't mean the old adage "Forgive and Forget." In fact, forgiving is *not* forgetting. How could we possibly forget the greatest hurts in our life? Forgiveness, instead, is choosing to no longer walk in the bondage of what others have done to us.

Know this: forgiveness is not a one-time thing to be accomplished. We may have survived deep hurts and trials of the past, but I can assure us all that there will be more in our future. Nobody is immune to hurt. Absolutely everyone reading this book has someone to forgive today or in the future. Let's not assume we are experts at forgiveness because we are familiar with the concept. Let's revisit the teachings of forgiveness as if we've never heard it before. It's dangerous to overlook an offense without forgiving, so we must get it right. This principle is for the past, the present, and the future and must be mastered.

WHAT JESUS SAYS ABOUT FORGIVENESS

Forgiveness is a principle widely accepted by Christians and non-Christians alike. We all have a moral compass in our hearts that knows when we have been wronged and that it must be made right. As a child, many of us were told, "Say you're sorry!" for whatever offense may have occurred. This likely accompanied an attitude in us that had no desire to seek forgiveness, but we went through the motions anyway to appease our parents (and likely sidestep any more punishment, if we're honest).

The reality is that forgiveness is widely known and is ingrained in us years before we truly begin to understand it. Forgiveness is like love. We all know about it, but we'd each give a different explanation for what it means. In the coming pages, we'll explore some common misnomers of forgiveness and establish a process of forgiveness, but first, let's start with the teachings that matter most: Jesus'.

> "Therefore, the kingdom of heaven is like a king who wanted to settle accounts with his servants. As he began the settlement, a man who owed him ten thousand bags of gold was brought to him. Since he was not able to pay, the master ordered that he and his wife and his children and all that he had be sold to repay the debt. "At this the servant fell on his knees before him. 'Be patient with me,' he begged, 'and I will pay back everything.' The servant's master took pity on him, canceled the debt and let him go. "But when that servant went out, he found one of his fellow servants who owed him a hundred silver coins. He grabbed him and began to choke him. 'Pay back what you owe me!' he demanded. "His fellow servant fell to his knees and begged him, 'Be patient with me, and I will pay it back.' "But he refused. Instead, he went off and had the man thrown into prison until he could pay the debt. When the other servants saw what had happened, they were outraged and went and told their master everything that had happened. "Then the master called the servant in. 'You wicked servant,' he said, 'I canceled all that debt of yours because you begged me to. Shouldn't you have had mercy on your fellow servant just as I had on you?' In anger his master handed him over to the jailers to be tortured, until he should pay back all he owed. "This is how my heavenly Father will treat each of you unless you forgive your

> brother or sister from your heart." (Matthew 18:23-35, NIV)

In this fictional story, Jesus clearly outlines the principle of forgiveness. We must remember when Jesus teaches a parable, His parables don't barely convey the truth, they are daggers of truth. I pray we uncover every piece of truth from this one.

There are 4+ characters in this story: the king, the servant, the servant's friend, and other servants. The King represents God and the servants represent humans. Notice, we've got a lot of servants in this story. Based on the cast list of this parable, we should expect that forgiveness largely deals with the people we rub shoulders with.

A servant borrows money from the king and now has to pay up. The servant didn't owe just a little bit of money either; he owes 10,000 bags of gold. This number is a significant debt. Just how big? A commentary in my Bible suggests that the debt was first described as 10,000 talents of gold - with one talent alone representing 20 years of a day laborer's wages. So, this servant owes 200,000 years of wages. This means that if I were to work every single day from the time that Jesus was alive until now, I would only have paid back 1% of what I owe. This is a *massive* debt! The servant owed an amount that is truly too great to fathom paying. So, the king informs his servant that there is no choice but to sell him and his family to pay for the debt. The entire price of the debt owed would fall on their heads.

Let's pause here. In this parable, we understand the king is God and the servants represent all types of humans. We must go one step further now. *You are the servant in great debt.* We have to put ourselves in this servant's place specifically. It matters not *how* the servant acquired such a great debt. The fact remains: it's time to pay up.

You and I are in great debt as well. Romans 3:23 says, "For the wages of sin is death, but the gift of God is eternal life in Christ Jesus our Lord" (NIV). The servant was completely responsible for the debt he owed, and the only way to justify it was with his life. *Just like us.* Thankfully, the king proves to be a very rich and good man.

The servant pleads forgiveness and the debt is forgiven. Can we even comprehend this? Again, we are this man. We owe a debt that is too great to be paid and then - just like that - we are free. 200,000 years given back to us. Praise God! When we hear that Jesus died for our sins, we must remember that we owed a debt too great to pay. We do not have 200,000 years to live to pay it off. So, this would be a pretty incredible day, right? If I were in the servant's sandals, I think I would go celebrate with my family and then maybe also sign up for Dave Ramsey's *Financial Peace University* to learn how to stay out of debt in the future. But this man does neither of those things.

The scripture says that as soon as he walked away from being forgiven, he found one of his servant friends who owed him money. While certainly not ideal to live in debt to each other, this fellow servant only owed 100 silver coins or 100 denarii, which translates to about 100 days of a laborer's wages. This is a reasonable debt; one that can certainly be repaid. But this fellow servant is not in a position to make the payment today. He pleads in the exact same way that the main servant of the story had just pleaded. Go back and read the text. He hears the very words he uttered maybe just an hour before - "Be patient with me, and I will pay it back." - but now, someone else is speaking them.

If we were listening to Jesus tell the story, we'd probably feel that He was leading to the happily ever after of this story; a loving conclusion where the servant happily forgives the debt that the fellow servant owed him because he was just forgiven a much greater debt. Right? Wrong. The hypocritical servant threw him in jail until he could pay it back. (As an aside, there is a deep irony here, because when he throws him in jail, the debtor is no longer able to make the money required to pay him back even if he wanted to. We see this a lot in real life when we give someone the cold shoulder until they apologize to us. Even if the other person *wanted* to apologize, our cold shoulder makes it nearly impossible to approach us.)

Back to the parable. The servant's reaction is obviously offensive to everyone listening. He was given an outlandish gift, undeservedly, only to turn around and deny a fellow servant even a portion of that same grace. Where is the justice? Well, justice arrived once the king found out. Swiftly, the debt that was just forgiven was reinstated. The king ordered the servant to be thrown in jail and tortured until he could pay it back. The justice is clear: the same measure of judgment the servant gave was now given to him. And that's the end for the servant. Once free, he will die in prison, chained to an unpayable debt.

The crowd listening to Jesus is now eerily silent. They are beginning to feel the foolishness of their own lives. There is a long pause. Nobody dares to speak. Jesus makes the point of the story crystal clear. "This is how my heavenly Father will treat each of you unless you forgive your brother or sister from your heart" (Matthew 18:35, NIV).

The parable is simply a story, but the point is very real. If there is any principle of forgiveness that we must fully understand, it's the measure we use toward others is the measure that is used on us. The grace - or lack thereof - we offer is the grace we will receive. Sure, we believe Jesus died for us and, of course, He did. But how are we forgiving after we have been forgiven? The main servant tasted true freedom, but lost it because he was unable to go and do likewise. Therefore, our ability to remain forgiven relies completely on our ability to forgive others. Think this is pretty harsh? Jesus doesn't hesitate.

> Do not judge, or you too will be judged. For in the same way you judge others, you will be judged, and with the measure you use, it will be measured to you. (Matthew 7:1-2, NIV)

> For if you forgive other people when they sin against you, your heavenly Father will also forgive you. But if you do not forgive others their sins, your Father will not forgive your sins. (Matthew 6:14-15, NIV)

> And when you stand praying, if you hold anything against anyone, forgive them, so that your Father in heaven may forgive you your sins. (Mark 11:25, NIV)

Paul even reminds us in Ephesians 4:32, "Be kind and compassionate to one another, forgiving each other, just as in Christ God forgave you" (NIV). In everything, Jesus reminds us as we take the gospel to the world that "Freely you have received; freely give" (Matthew 10:8, NIV). Forgiveness is a free gift. We cannot do anything to earn it, but we *can* do something to lose it. There is one way we can lose the forgiveness of God - *and that is by not forgiving others.*

When I grew up in church, I remember the weight that one prayer carried. "Jesus, please forgive me of my sins and come into my heart." Everyone around me assured me that this little prayer is all it takes, and I would certainly be saved from my sins. But years later, in all honesty, I struggle with that promise in light of what I just read in the Bible. When I read all the verses listed above, the truth seems to state that we are forgiven to the level we forgive others. If there is someone we haven't forgiven, then we are not forgiven. Yes, this may seem harsh, but it is only harsh because we have been taught an incomplete gospel that hasn't required us to "go and do likewise" (see Luke 10:37). The "go and do likewise" has to do with showing mercy to others. Forgiveness has been taught more as a suggestion than as a condition for salvation. Friends, this is a big deal! We must have a clear understanding and practice of forgiveness. There is only one thing that can stand in the way of our forgiveness from God and that is the way we forgive others.

You may say, "But Caleb, you don't understand how badly I have been hurt." Listen, we can certainly compare hurts and share scars. Your pain is real. Your hurt is heard. *There is still hope.* Let me remind you: 200,000 years... two hundred thousand! 73 million days in debt. Yes, we have all experienced different levels of pain and hardship. And yet: no pain will ever be greater than the sin we have caused. We deserve to die for our sins. If you've never asked God to forgive you of your sins, you have the weight of the world on your shoulders. Daily, you are carrying around your own punishment, an eternal death. But many of us *have* asked for God's forgiveness. And we still feel the weight of the world on our shoulders. So, what gives?

I asked Jesus to forgive me and come into my life in 6th grade at a summer camp. But that's not the end of my story. Now, I have to go and do the same. I have to forgive. The reality of the story Jesus told was that the servant - you and I - had tasted forgiveness, but by the end of the story, he found himself in jail for the same debt he was once forgiven of. Why? Because the king - God - is not pleased when He gives a gift that is quickly forgotten and not passed on.

And this is the very problem we find ourselves in. We will all be hurt by others. That is not the *real* problem. The real problem is that we have forgotten the debt in which we owed. Whose sins put Jesus on the cross? If we even for a moment forget that it was yours and mine, then we will easily slip and become the hypocrite that doesn't forgive after being forgiven a greater debt. When does forgiveness get easier? When we recognize that no one is in need of forgiveness as much as we ourselves are. The victory of forgiveness can only come through God. We cannot forgive others unless we have first been forgiven, but to stay free, we have to remember the cross. The servant forgot, and it cost him everything.

HOW DO I KNOW I NEED TO FORGIVE?

If you are bitter, anxious, or fearful, the cause may be - and likely is - unforgiveness. How could I make such a bold statement? Well, look at a baby. Are they born bitter, anxious, or fearful? No. We become these things after we have experienced a hurt in our life. Someone we loved and trusted hurt us, usually pretty early on in our life. It could have been intentional; it could have been unintentional. The reason doesn't matter as much as the fact: we were hurt. If it was an isolated instance, we probably aren't too wounded. If it was a repeated hurt, we probably have some serious wounds that, left open, may lead to greater problems in other areas of our life. But no matter what our current problem is, if we are feeling bitter, fearful, and/or anxious, we must take a look at our heart to see if we're harboring any unforgiveness - yes, even as far back as childhood. If we prioritize forgiveness, we'll be surprised by everything that comes next - a lightness in our heart, a renewal in our spirit, a song in our soul.

WHO DO I NEED TO FORGIVE?

We may know who we need to forgive if someone is praised in front of us and we secretly cringe in disgust. Or, if we dodge someone we don't like in the grocery store. Or, if we avoid a particular neighbor. (Whether you're an extrovert or an introvert, avoiding for *any* reason may be rooted in unforgiveness.) Or, we may be having a great day and everything is going well until the thought of a person or situation that hurt us in the past pops into our head and our day is ruined. If we find ourselves making excuses for why something didn't actually hurt us, we may need to forgive. The measure I personally use to know if I need to forgive is that if someone walks in while I am preaching and I change the way I preach or fixate on them, I need to forgive.

Check your pulse right now. If you have a pulse, you likely need to forgive. Feel like you're all caught up on forgiving others? Well, it's kind of what people like to say about the weather here in Indiana; just wait a couple hours and that will change. Don't try to avoid pain, just get good at learning to forgive.

HELP ME FORGIVE

I want to finish our chapter together discussing the practical ways we can walk in forgiveness. We must do each of these steps in order. If we skip one, or go out of order, we will make this process so much harder, if not impossible.

STEP 1 – REPENT

Before we can forgive someone else, we have to be forgiven. After all, how can we give something that we have never received? The major key to walking in forgiveness is to remember our own forgiveness. When John the Baptist came to prepare the way for Jesus, of all the lofty concepts and life-changing directives he could have preached about, he chose repentance. "Repent, for the kingdom of heaven has come near" (Matthew 3:2, NIV). Jesus' first message echoed the same (see Matthew 4:17). If we want the Kingdom of Heaven to be near, we must repent. *The nearness of heaven is directly associated with a repentant heart.* If we feel distant from Christ, we must truly ask ourselves if we have repented of our sins.

Repentance is a change of direction. It's not just saying, "Lord, I am sorry." It's saying, "Lord, I am sorry," and then changing our ways. I know this is easier said than done. Thankfully, there is no limit to how many times we can ask God to forgive us. In fact, the only barrier occurs when we have stopped asking altogether. If there is anything God desires for us to repent over, it's probably less our pet peeve of a sin and probably more our forgetfulness of the depths from which we have been saved. Think back to the parable. The king did not seem upset about the amount of debt he had to forgive. The king was willing to forgive the debt no matter what. The debt could have been everything under the sun. God, too, is capable and desires to forgive every one of our sins under the sun. But we must ask, and we must repent. Wherever we are today, we must humble ourselves and speak to Jesus directly. Tell Him you are sorry for the life you are living, and - *mostly* - for forgetting about what He did to save you.

When it comes to personal repentance, we are arriving at this path from one of two roads: (1) We have never repented for our sins, or (2) we are repenting for forgetting to repent. Let's address the first.

Romans 10:9-10 says, "If you declare with your mouth, "Jesus is Lord," and believe in your heart that God raised him from the dead, you will be saved. For it is with your heart that you believe and are justified, and it is with your mouth that you profess your faith and are saved" (NIV). As simply as the servant begged the king to forgive him, so simply is it for us to plead our guilt to God and ask Him to forgive us. It isn't our good deeds that save us; it is *His* good deed that saves us. "For it is by grace you have been saved, through faith—and this is not from yourselves, it is the gift of God—not by works, so that no one can boast" (Ephesians 2:8-9, NIV). God wants all the glory to Himself. Therefore, salvation requires nothing but our willing heart to proclaim Jesus as Lord and believe God raised Him from the dead.

Now, if we are someone that has professed to be a born-again Christian, but we haven't been passing on forgiveness to others, we need to go back to the king and beg for forgiveness again. We had been forgiven the debt, but based on our actions, we are back in a lot of debt. The reason the king in the story threw the servant in prison to be tortured to repay the debt is because he was using the same measure of judgment that the servant used on his fellow servant. The king didn't torture him because he wanted to; he did it because it was just. We can go back to the king and plead again and follow-up quickly by showing we forgive those around us. My ask of us all is to never feel too distant to run back to God. God asks us to forgive others an unlimited number of times because that's how He treats each of us. We just have to keep falling on our knees.

There is no limit to the number of times we can repent. The more, the better. It doesn't matter if this is the first time or 200,000th time. Take a moment to repent again. My dad taught me that repentance doesn't just get us back to square one, but actually launches us further ahead of where we would've been. God certainly seems to value the repentant heart. Oftentimes, it is helpful to physically get on our knees or lay face down on the floor as a posture of lowering oneself before God. God will come near to the broken hearted and to those who walk in forgiveness.

STEP 2 – INVITE THE HELPER

When Jesus left earth to go to heaven, He promised that He would send a helper to be with us and to remind us of everything He taught. This is the Holy Spirit! Any quest to be completely free from unforgiveness on our own is a futile journey. We need help. We need someone that can scan our hearts and know us better than we do. This is especially important as we work to forgive our deepest pains.

The mind is powerful. When humans experience a deep amount of trauma, we cope with that pain by attempting to forget it entirely. It is not uncommon to ask someone to describe a deep pain in their life and to receive a vague response in return, as if the details are buried well beneath the grief. Whether our pain is on the forefront of our mind or not, it is equally destructive. How could we know the intricacies of the human heart? Your heart? We have to ask the Holy Spirit to bring to the surface the hurts we need to forgive. This is a must.

The prayer can go something like this: "Holy Spirit, I need help. Teach me to forgive others like Jesus forgave me. Please bring to mind any person or situation that I have left unforgiven in my heart." When we pray this prayer, we should do it in a quiet place with plenty of space for the Holy Spirit to answer that prayer. Don't force anything. Just relax and continue on to step 3.

STEP 3 – MAKE A LIST

When we pray to ask the Holy Spirit to remind us of areas we have left unforgiven in our hearts, we must make sure to give ourselves some time alone. I suggest blocking at least an hour. We may not need all that time, but most people are surprised by what is uncovered in this process. I suggest not having much else to do right after surfacing our deep hurts either.

As the Holy Spirit speaks to us, memories might surface. I want you to jot down on a piece of paper any person or situation that comes to mind. Don't try to analyze the situation or person at this moment; just try to uncover a list of places God wants you to forgive.

Write down any thoughts or memories that come to mind.

Let's not allow ourselves to give an excuse for why we don't or shouldn't write something down. Just write. We may even remember things that we feel like we've already forgiven. Write it down anyway. Just trust the Holy Spirit to do His thing. It's possible we may have forgiven parts of situations, but God wants total forgiveness - a debt paid in full.

We shouldn't feel ashamed by the number of people or situations we have on our list. Whether we have 2, 22, or 2,000, it doesn't matter: nothing compares to the sins we have been forgiven. Let's not fall victim to pride if we only think of one and, likewise, let's not allow self-condemnation if we have more than we thought we should. The beauty is in the progression. This list is where that progress begins.

STEP 4 – DON'T RUSH

Seeing a list of all the hurts in our life is quite overwhelming. It's okay to feel a wide range of emotions at this moment. Can I add a couple more things to everyone's list? If we didn't put ourselves or God on the list, we would be wise to add them now. Oftentimes, we are our own worst enemy. How can we love someone and hate someone so much? But we experience this duality with ourselves all the time, and honestly, many of us experience these same conflicting feelings with God. Even though God has never done anything wrong, we sometimes need to forgive our perceptions of God. God is unchanged by our ideas of Him, but *we* are deeply impacted. Forgiving God will give us a fresh start to rediscover Him again and eliminate false beliefs that we have held from the past.

Once we have our list, don't rush to forgive them all. Let's take our time to heal and forgive. Forgiveness is not a split-second thing. The hurts we have on that list have occurred over a lifetime, so let's give ourselves some time to work through them, one at a time. Pick a single name, or the people involved in a single situation, and move on to steps 5-7.

STEP 5 – WRITE THE WRONG

This is where things get sticky, but don't give up. Grab a piece of paper or find a place to type, and I want you to write down all the hurts this one person has caused you. We needn't be logical here. Just write down whatever you're feeling. It is normal for some of the hurt we have in our hearts to not have any basis in reality. So what? We have to deal with the pain that actually occurred *as well as the pain we perceive in our minds*. Write it all out in detail. What happened that hurt you? The closer the individual is to us, the longer the list. (Spoiler alert: our longest list is probably for ourselves.)

Start by writing at the top "I forgive ___________ for:" Fill in the name of the person here, or the people involved in a situation. Then, underneath, write out the reasons you need to forgive them. Write out all your hurts. Be specific and don't make excuses for the person - or for you. Try to distinctly write out all the feelings and reasons you have. Don't just say, "I forgive Caleb for being apathetic." Say, "I forgive Caleb for not being excited for me when I aced my test." Put all your dirty laundry on this paper. It is not for others to see and it will be quickly destroyed in a few steps.

In some cases, the pain someone has caused began with an initial catalyst but is now an ongoing part of your life. No amount of forgiveness will fix what happened. Let's imagine I am hit by a drunk driver and I am left paralyzed. I have to forgive the driver for being irresponsible on that night, and I also have to forgive the ongoing suffering that I will have for the rest of my life. We have to acknowledge all of it to forgive it. It is possible to forgive even though we may always face the repercussions of what was done to us. Again, do this step alone and with some time to process.

STEP 6 – CHOOSE FORGIVENESS

With our list of hurts in hand, we have to make a conscious decision to choose forgiveness. Forgiveness is not a feeling; it is a choice of the will. In this step, we turn from our emotions and choose to follow the example of Jesus by forgiving the way we have been forgiven. I want you to read your list of grievances against that person *out loud.* Start with the top. "I forgive ______ for..." and read aloud each and every hurt.

It's okay to cry. It's okay to feel nothing. This is an act of obedience. We have chosen forgiveness, and I believe forgiveness is accomplished at this moment. However, we may not feel as free as we might like to be.

STEP 7 – PRAY BLESSING

This step is where freedom comes. We now throw away, burn, rip up, or delete our pieces of paper with our list of specific hurts on it. We have verbally expressed our choice to forgive. We are moving on. Now, start a new paper. On this paper, we are going to write a prayer for the individual we just forgave. This is not a prayer to ask God to fix all of their faults. Instead, we pray a prayer of blessing for that person. Pray their job is blessed. Pray their marriage is blessed. Pray their kids adore them. Pray they become the star on their team. Pray they acquire great wealth. Pray anything good and blessed and holy and righteous you can think of. Write this down on a piece of paper and pray the prayer every day.

The trick is that we pray this prayer of blessing every day until we associate the person with our prayer of blessing, not the hurt they caused us. It doesn't mean we have to be best friends with the person or even ever talk to them again. We just have to free our mind of the bitterness we've clinged to. This process could potentially take a few minutes, 3 days or 6 months - or longer. You will get there. You will be free. You can be free.

When I was in high school, my dad and I weren't getting along. It seemed like we were always setting each other off and causing hurt to each other. Finally, we went to see another pastor for counseling. Seated in the middle of Pizza Hut, faster than any of us could say "Pepperoni, please," the pastor said, "I don't really care what your problem is; we are going to work on moving on." He told us to write a letter to each other every day for three weeks. In the letter, we were to write something about each other that we were thankful for, and something about each other that we admired. No corrections; just kindness. Twenty-one letters later, we have never looked back. God knew my dad and I needed to be together - both then, and now. As of the writing of this book, my dad and I have worked at the same church now for over 4 years and every bit of The Rejuvenation Project has been birthed in that time. What if I held on to my bitterness? I would be scared to wonder what my life would be had I not chosen to forgive.

The enemy tried to sever our relationship using the tool of unforgiveness. How did we fight it? With blessing and kindness, the same way you and I can with every other relationship snag we encounter. If I didn't work through the pain to offer blessing, my relationship with my father would be damaged to this day. In fact, it is my belief that, as a result, this very book would never have been written.

STEP 8 – REPEAT

After we complete that process for one person - whether it took a week or a year - go back to the list and pick a new name of a person or the people involved in a situation and repeat steps 5-7 of the process. The more we start walking in forgiveness rather than bitterness, the more we may notice that the process goes faster for each individual we choose to forgive. This is a good sign. We are beginning to experience the freedom that comes with forgiveness.

MISCELLANEOUS TIPS

You may be wondering why the process of forgiveness doesn't include a conversation with the person or people involved in your painful situation. Forgiveness is a process that can be completely accomplished *without the person who hurt you*. If the person who hurt you is a close relative or spouse who is repeatedly causing pain to you, this would warrant a conversation on future boundaries to prevent further hurts, sure. But a conversation is not necessary for you to forgive them. Most of the time, the person doesn't realize they hurt you.

A word of caution: Do not walk up to someone and tell them you decided to forgive them. This will only create tension with the other person. In the rare instance a person apologizes, sure, say you forgive them. However, do not hold your breath for this to happen. Your capacity to forgive does not hinge on their capacity to apologize. If, in this process, you realize the pain you have caused to others, a genuine and humble apology goes a long way. This can be face to face, or a handwritten letter. If you just feel guilty over a situation you caused and have already apologized, you shouldn't keep apologizing. If guilt persists, you need to forgive yourself going through the steps of forgiveness, rather than continue apologizing to someone else.

Many times, this process of forgiveness can be accomplished on your own. However, if this process seems paralyzing, I would encourage you to reach out to your pastor or a Christian counselor and ask them to help you process and walk in forgiveness. Under no circumstances is there a hurt too big to forgive. I want to say that as compassionately as I can. Yes, there are bigger hurts out there than I can imagine, but nothing compares to the debt Jesus forgave us. We can forgive it all because Jesus forgave it all.

THE REJUVENATION PROJECT

Walk through these steps so you can be free from unforgiveness and experience the freedom of truly being forgiven. This chapter is crucial to rejuvenation because the list of people who hurt you will be added to *for the rest of your life.* The key to staying rejuvenated is to not let people stay on your list for a long time. Even this week, I have had to forgive someone. However, I went through this process in 20 minutes rather than months because I didn't linger in the bitterness. This practice has become a cornerstone habit, and with practice, over time, it becomes second nature. Use this process to stay free for your life and maintain the forgiveness Jesus offers us all.

CHAPTER EIGHT

PURPOSE

IF WE FEEL like we are lacking in an area of our life, more than likely we lack purpose. And I don't just mean wandering through life without direction. If we are lacking in righteousness, kindness, confidence, love, or anything else it will stem from a lack of purpose. The great evangelist Billy Sunday once said, "More people fail from lack of purpose than from lack of talent."[8] Purpose gives direction and meaning to life which allows for wisdom, blessing and satisfaction to flourish. Truthfully, it's impossible for any of us to lack purpose because every person in existence was given a purpose by God. Therefore, the problem is less a purpose problem and more finding a clear vision of that purpose.

Our purpose is the root system of our life. If we don't like the fruit our life is producing, we likely aren't living in the purpose we were made for. But in the daily distractions of a busy life, we can't always see our purpose. From time to time, our purpose seems hidden from us, and we lack the clear vision to find it. Proverbs 29:18 says, "Where there is no vision, the people perish: but he that keepeth the law, happy is he" (KJV).

Sin issues are often just issues stemming from a clouded vision of our purpose. If we're struggling with a deeply-rooted problem in our life, whether it's recurring outbursts of anger or broken promises or a porn addiction, I'd venture to guess the root isn't so much a character flaw as it is a vision flaw. We're not seeking sin on purpose; we're seeking sin because we're not living on purpose. There is a difference. How do we know what our God given purpose is? The good news: we have already been given this gift from God. It is not our job to create it. It is our job to *find* it.

Our purpose is found at the intersection of our passions, abilities, gifts and experiences and what God is doing in the world. The intersection is key. To simply live by our passions, abilities, gifts and experiences without knowing what God is doing in the world will leave us productive, but unfulfilled. Knowing what God is doing in the world, but not living by our passions, abilities, gifts and experiences will leave us religiously prideful, but burdened. Unsurprisingly, both paths lead to burnout. We're left crushed by the weight of the world.

Ready for a quick science lesson? The earth's atmosphere weighs 14.7 pounds per square inch at sea level. This means the average person - you and I - has the weight of a car pressing down on us *at all times*.[9] So how are we not crushed by this tremendous weight? Because we were created with a constant, continuous flow of pressure inside our bodies that presses back to equalize our surroundings. We can walk, talk, swim, jump, and move through life as if there is no weight on us all, because *what is inside of us is perfectly designed for what is outside of us.* Many of us have never stopped to notice we have the weight of a car on top of us because we were created to carry it. We walk around feeling completely free and unobstructed.

This is the best way to describe purpose. There is a place for us in this world that will leave us feeling completely free, even under a tremendous weight. It's our purpose: the intersection that occurs when what God has put in us perfectly matches His plan outside of us. If we have a tremendous weight on our shoulders to perform certain duties or if we are consistently stressed and overwhelmingly anxious, then what is outside of us is bigger than what God has put inside of us and we likely need to cut back. Alternately, if we are feeling like our life isn't all it's cracked up to be and we feel we were made for more than this, we're right: we are living with a great deal of internal pressure because God *did* make us for more, and our depth and capacity needs to be matched with the circumstances outside of us. Living in our purpose is often described as feeling balanced, and in a sense, it is. We're equalizing the pressure within us to the world beyond us.

Sounds simple, but how do we get there? We may be surprised to find out that we are not so far off from becoming aligned with God's purpose. In fact, we can fulfill our purpose wherever we are today. But there are two absolutes to consider when searching for the purpose of our life: (1) it's not our job to choose or invent our purpose, and (2) our complete purpose does not exist on this earth.

First, God made us. The less we believe that, the harder it will be to find any real purpose for our life. The prophet Isaiah says, "What sorrow awaits those who argue with their Creator. Does a clay pot argue with its maker? Does the clay dispute with the one who shapes it, saying, 'Stop, you're doing it wrong!' Does the pot exclaim, 'How clumsy can you be?'" (Isaiah 45:9, NLT). Can we just go ahead and release the pressure to create ourselves? We have all heard the phrase, "I am a self-made man." Oh, how wicked of a statement. It is not up to us to choose or invent our identity or purpose. It is as foolish as the clay telling the potter what to do. God, our creator, has given humans the ability to create and define countless things in the world, but our identities and purposes are not on that list. Friends, this is great news! I have a hard enough time choosing what to have for breakfast, so thank God I don't have to choose my purpose too.

Second, the Kingdom of Heaven isn't just advanced here on earth; it is also advanced in heaven. When we live on this earth, we really just give God a chance to evaluate us before we step into our eternal destinies. I have yet to meet a person who feels like they've accomplished all they were made for. The reason? There is more for them in the next life! This shouldn't make us slack on our purpose today, but rather we should find more satisfaction in it, both today and tomorrow because it will live on *forever*. Jesus says in Luke 16:10-12:

> Whoever can be trusted with very little can also be trusted with much, and whoever is dishonest with very little will also be dishonest with much. So if you have not been trustworthy in handling worldly wealth, who will trust you with true riches? And if you have not been trustworthy with someone else's property, who will give you property of your own? (NIV)

Notice the use of the words "worldly" and "true." The meaning is clear: What we have in this world is borrowed and isn't all that real. While the parable seems to address money, I believe the same could be said of our purpose. If we cannot live in the plan God has for us on earth, how will He trust us to carry out His ways in heaven? There is a life to come that is more real than this one. Our purpose is ultimately for that place, not here. Plan accordingly. Play the long game. We shouldn't get nearsighted and frustrated when everything about our life doesn't make sense today, right this very minute.

No matter how hard we try, we can search all throughout this earth and never come to our true purpose because our true purpose is for more than this earth. This is okay - good, even - because we will have all of eternity to keep seeking it out. Our purpose will not end when our life on earth does. Let's just keep learning a little more about what God has put inside of us each day. This is the work of a faithful servant.

I was once coaching a young woman who has an incredible gift for worship and singing. Everyone in her life could acknowledge this fact, yet it baffled her to wonder how this should be used for God in this world. Was she to start a music career? Maybe, but this is too nearsighted. I told her that God didn't give her a gift to make a song on iTunes. He made her to lead worship for the multitudes in heaven. Now instead of preparing for just a music career on earth, she is stewarding a purpose that will actually impact heaven. Her platform may not come on this earth, but it will likely come before the feet of Jesus. Now she can sing to Jesus alone in her house and not have to worry if she is squandering a gift God gave her. Her talent is for more than earth. When we imagine our purpose impacting heaven, we are able to maintain a healthy perspective of our lives and what God has called us to do. Our true purpose should always lead us to a bigger perspective of God and His Kingdom, not a smaller one.

WHEN WE'VE BEEN THERE 10,000 YEARS

One way we can know we have properly identified our God-given purpose is that it will not change over time. A true purpose from God will be the same today as it will be 10,000 years from today. One of the best questions to ask the Holy Spirit when inquiring about our purpose is: "Holy Spirit, what is my job in heaven?"

Work was created before Eve ate the forbidden fruit that opened the door to sin. This means that work is a part of God's perfect creation, and thus, can be expected in heaven. While sin caused work to become toil, it was not this way from the beginning. We will work in heaven. If we ask the Holy Spirit what we will do there, we can better prepare and live in that purpose today. The Kingdom of our God is not just advanced on earth, it is being advanced everywhere at all times. We will have a role to play, both as mortals and beyond.

As a pastor, if I believe my job is to help people become free from sin, I will have missed my God-given purpose. There is no sin in heaven, so helping people get free from sin cannot be my sole purpose today and in 10,000 years. I asked God one day, "What's my job in heaven?" He said: *Teach people how to live in heaven.* I haven't been to heaven, but it is not unrealistic to believe there might be a need for someone to teach people the ways of eternal life in the presence of God. And while I can't yet know exactly what that work will look like in eternity, I *can* start learning to live that purpose today. My job on earth is to teach people how to live in heaven. A large portion of my life, therefore, is dedicated to (1) learning how to live in heaven and (2) teaching it, whether I am at home or at work. I have found great joy and satisfaction living this out each day.

Your purpose won't be my purpose, but I can assure you that God isn't trying to hide it from you. Begin to ask Him about it. When you discover something that can be done today as well as 10,000 years from today, you have found your destiny.

DIRT + BREATH OF GOD = HUMANITY

With the foundational wisdom in place that we don't create our purpose and it will not end on earth, we can truly begin to search out our purpose. As with any form of discovery, we'll use the power of observation. What are we made out of? Scripture says we were created from dust and brought to life with the breath of God (Genesis 2:7). We have the structure of dirt, and we have the breath of an eternal creator inside of us. This is why life gets confusing at times: some of it feels so important and some of it just feels like dirt! When I started my first job as a pastor, my dad told me, "50% of your job is eternal and 50% is just a job. Don't confuse the two." The breath of God is intertwined with dirt. Blessed are the people who properly call dirt, "dirt" and the breath of God, "the breath of God." This means that our earthly purpose has both finite qualities and eternal qualities at the same time. Let me clarify.

When we think of purpose, we think of action. Purpose is doing and accomplishing. But surely that's not all it is, right? What can we do that God can't? What can we accomplish that He hasn't already? God can do anything. He is bigger and stronger and mightier than us all. So, what would a big God need from us that He couldn't already do Himself? Love Him. Jesus teaches it better than I do:

> As Jesus and his disciples were on their way, he came to a village where a woman named Martha opened her home to him. She had a sister called Mary, who sat at

> the Lord's feet listening to what he said. But Martha was distracted by all the preparations that had to be made. She came to him and asked, "Lord, don't you care that my sister has left me to do the work by myself? Tell her to help me!" "Martha, Martha," the Lord answered, "you are worried and upset about many things, but few things are needed—or *indeed only one.* Mary has chosen what is better, and it will not be taken away from her. (Luke 10:38-42, NIV)

These two women had a heart to love and serve Jesus. One chose to sit at His feet and listen; the other decided to be hospitable and make preparations to her house to serve. Jesus didn't say one way was right and the other was wrong. He simply said the woman that sat at His feet and listened did what is *better*.

What I find most impactful is when Jesus says, "few things are needed—or indeed only one." There is just one thing needed! Jesus, the Lord Almighty, makes it distinctly clear that He doesn't need people to do things for Him because he is perfectly capable of that. He is looking for people who can do the only thing that He can't: to sit at His feet and listen. Both of these verbs, *sit* and *listen,* are not very action oriented. They don't feel very purposeful. But, in fact, that's exactly what God wants from us in this life: to sit and listen to Him.

Sounds easy enough, right? But in America, we are good at moving and talking - getting things done. The usual excuse for why we can't sit and listen at the feet of Jesus is because we are movin' and shakin'. "I just don't have time." "I am too busy." "I have to fight the injustices of our world." We've got a lot of busy bodies. A lot of talking heads. And a whole lot of nothing to show for it. I know it sounds contrary to our sinful nature, but sitting and listening *is* the purpose of man. And wherever a God-given purpose is, an enemy prowls just around the bend. I feel more confident that our mission on this earth is to sit and listen to God because it's obvious how strongly the enemy fights us to make time for it.

King Solomon says it like this, "Fear God and keep his commandments, for this is the duty of all mankind" (Ecclesiastes 12:13, NIV). You may have heard the phrase "paralyzed by fear." Whenever someone in the scriptures had an encounter with God or an angel, they were often struck with fear and either didn't move or fell to the ground. The presence of God halts us in our tracks. If we fear God, we will sit. To keep God's commandments, we first have to listen to them. The sole duty of mankind is to fear God and keep his commandments. To be still and listen. He just needs us to be with Him.

I have often wondered what I will regret when I stand before Jesus. That is not to say that when we stand before Jesus, we are filled with regret. It is just a personal thought I have had. To this day, when I think about that question, the only thing I can picture regretting as I stand before Jesus is "Why didn't I pray more?" I am convinced that I will not be thinking about church attendance, sports championships, straight A's, the money in my investment portfolio, or my addictions when I see Jesus. No, the thing I would regret is, "Why didn't I sit with You more?"

Purpose is found at the intersection of our passions, gifts, abilities, and experiences and what God is doing in the world. You know which of those roads is harder to identify? What God is doing in the world. We have a lot of tests and inventories to help people learn about themselves, but there is only one way to know what God is doing and that is to sit at His feet.

The goal of The Rejuvenation Project is to make our last days on earth our best days with Christ. That with the dawn of each new day we are more on fire for the Lord. That we're continually moving forward, exponentially growing, running the race to finish strong. Sitting and listening to God is a huge part of fulfilling that desire. I want for us to arrive in heaven and pick up our conversation with Jesus where it left off just minutes ago. I do not want us to see our creator after decades of not talking to Him and feeling full of guilt and shame. Our job, today and for all of our lives, is to sit and listen.

PURPOSE AND CAREER

One thing that usually trips us up the most when it comes to purpose is that we use the term "purpose" and "career" interchangeably. Our purpose is not our career and our career is not our purpose. A career is how people make money; a purpose is what people live for. None of us were made to live for money. This is good news! If we have a career problem and are feeling stuck in a dead-end job, it doesn't necessarily imply we're living out the wrong purpose. Maybe we just want a different way to make money? But if we have a purpose problem, everything in our life will suffer.

It is pretty common to hear that as soon as a person gives their life to Jesus and falls in love with Him, they start wondering if they should quit their job to work in full-time ministry. I've even heard of people who hesitate to give their life to Jesus because they don't want to become a pastor! But just because we love Jesus doesn't mean we need to be a pastor or a missionary. We don't need to be in full-time ministry to love God. Often, I meet people who love Jesus wholeheartedly and aren't in formal ministry, and, all too often, I meet people in formal ministry and wonder if they've ever even met Jesus. The key for purpose is not to do what we think we should do with our life. The key is to do what God thinks we should do with our life.

WHAT CAREER WAS I MADE TO DO?

First of all, if you sped through that section on Mary and Martha just to get to the part where I help you find purpose in action, then you've already missed it. Let me say it again: *there is nothing better in this life than to sit and listen to Jesus!* When we do, the Lord directs our path. With every twist and turn, we receive direction. His Word is a lamp unto our feet and a light unto our path. In purpose and life, we needn't second-guess or doubt or fumble in the dark. Jesus will guide our ways.

Picture a car. Be it gas or electric, that car was designed to be powerful, fast, comfortable, and efficient. However, if that car never revisits the gas tank or the charging station, it is useless. We are like that car and God is our source of power, purpose, and guidance. If we don't consistently revisit Him to sit and listen, we are empty, fuelless, and futile. Regardless of the equipment on board, a car is only good if it has the power to move. We must be filled up! And our human range calls for far more capacity than a gas tank. If we go more than a day without sitting and listening to Jesus, we will not operate the way we were made.

Now notice, in this chapter I have given two definitions for my purpose in life: (1) *sit and listen at Jesus' feet* and (2) *teach people how to live in heaven*. So, which is truly my purpose? God doesn't often comply with our desire for one nice and tidy definition. Both are my purpose and both must be pursued in tandem.

We see this concept of tandem pursuit exemplified in the building of the tabernacle. We often skip over these chapters in the early part of the Bible where a lot of Bible reading plans go to die (Exodus, Leviticus, Numbers, and Deuteronomy). The tabernacle maintained seven pieces of furniture, and of those seven, there was a table of showbread and a lampstand. Stick with me here. Within the tabernacle, the table of showbread was on the north wall and the lampstand was on the south wall. Whereas everything else in the tabernacle was sequential for encountering the presence of God, the table of showbread and the golden lampstand worked hand-in-hand. They stood right across from each other. In short, the table of showbread represents communion with God and the lampstand represents Jesus, the light of the world, as we are to be a light to the world (Matthew 5:14).

We must note: where the ministry of the table was present, the ministry of the lamp was present, and where the ministry of the lamp was present, the ministry of the table was present. These two were inseparable, a tandem representation. The table is the intimate relationship with God that fuels the work of ministry. And the work of ministry fuels deeper understanding and stronger bonds in our relationship with God.

In my life specifically, the more I sit and listen to God, the more

I understand heaven to be able to teach it. The more I teach about heaven, the more I love and desire spending time with the Father. It's a never-ending cycle. We all have the same purpose to sit with God and listen to Him, but where He sends us to be the light of the world is up to Him. The ministry we perform should flow from our time with God and our time of ministry should encourage a greater desire to dwell with God. If we find that combo and work within it, we will find the deepest satisfaction in life.

I was in high school when God first told me why He made me. I didn't understand it was God's voice at the time. Now, I look back and realize it was one of the clearest things He has ever said to me. I was at a church camp and we were worshiping. I was sitting in a chair listening to the music during a service when God spoke directly to my spirit: *I made you to lead my church.* My first thought was "I don't want to be a pastor." However, as my brain was saying no, my spirit was coming alive. I remember finally saying "Yes!" I lifted my hands as high in the air as I could and I was overcome by the Holy Spirit of God.

At that time, I felt I had two choices: be a senior pastor or a youth pastor. That's all I knew. I figured I should be a senior pastor since I felt God say that I was supposed to lead His church. In my own skewed, 17-year-old mind, a senior pastor sounded way more important than a youth pastor. But I had a long while to go before I would start doing what God made me to do.

Flash forward three years later. I was attending Ball State University, leading Bible studies and chapels on my baseball team. I was sitting and preparing a Bible study in the recreation center when the Spirit of God spoke again: *You aren't a pastor when you get paid to do it. You are a pastor because I told you.* Since I was 17, I believed that I was not doing what I was made to do because I wasn't paid for it yet. That day, I realized I was a pastor on my baseball team. I wasn't getting paid for it, but I was doing it because it was what God made me for.

My dad, also a pastor, had a similar experience in high school when God called him to lead the church. He describes being overcome with the Spirit of God as God called him to ministry. He finished high school, went to college, went to seminary, and did the work to become an ordained pastor. It took ten years for man to finally confirm what God had already decided. My dad says that when God touched his heart in high school, he was moved by power. When a bishop announced him as an ordained pastor, the effect held little power at all.

Friends, we get our unique purpose when God gives it to us. This is why sitting and listening is *vital*. We can achieve the best things in the world, but if God didn't start it, we will work incredibly hard and have very little satisfaction or fruit from our work. At the same time, if God speaks purpose to us, even if no man believes it, we can accomplish immeasurably more than we could ask or imagine. God made us first for Himself. Whatever He asks us to do from there is His choice. Our job is to just sit, listen, and obey any time he asks us to do something.

A lot of times, people in ministry think everything they do within the church walls is the Lord's work. On the flip side, I have met people who work in the marketplace that believe none of what they do is important because it isn't church work. Whether we are the pope, a janitor, a stay-at-home parent, or anything else: we are in a body of dust, filled with the breath of God. No matter who we are. No matter what we do. Part of our life or career can be eternal, and part of it is just life. We must never confuse the two. But how? How do we know what is eternal and what is just this life?

"So, whether you eat or drink or whatever you do, do it all for the glory of God" (1 Corinthians 10:31, NIV). God is not impressed by what we do because He can always do better. He is not impressed by the outward stuff. He is impressed with the *heart*. 1 Samuel 16:7 says, "The LORD does not look at the things people look at. People look at the outward appearance, but the LORD looks at the heart" (NIV). So how do we know what will be eternally rewarded and what is just from the earth? Well, it's mostly our choice. Whatever heart we bring to something will determine whether it is used for God's ultimate purpose or if it will scatter like dust.

> "Not everyone who says to me, 'Lord, Lord,' will enter the kingdom of heaven, but only the one who does the will of my Father who is in heaven. Many will say to me on that day, 'Lord, Lord, did we not prophesy in your name and in your name drive out demons and in your name perform many miracles?' Then I will tell them plainly, 'I never knew you. Away from me, you evildoers!'" (Matthew 7:21-23, NIV)

This passage clearly shows that good works are not the measuring rod for God's ways. Some followers drove out demons that were against God Himself. They prophesied in His name, and performed actual *miracles*. Surely these miraculous acts prove that these people were living for the purpose of God, right? But God is not impressed by what we do; He is impressed by those He knows. He knows us if we sit and listen at His feet. This is why many of us have a hard time understanding what we were made for. We assume the perfect career exists somewhere out there, and we search forever to find it. All this time, it's right under our feet. Or rather, at Jesus'.

I have been both an unfulfilled pastor and a fulfilled pastor at different times in my life. At the first church I worked at, I was a youth pastor leading middle school and high schoolers. I never truly felt fulfilled. So, I moved to a new city and took a new job as a youth pastor leading middle school and high schoolers. I felt completely in my element. Same exact career. Two different satisfactions. The difference came when I regularly started sitting and listening to God. At my first job, I did what I thought was expected of me. At my second job, I do what God expects of me. The problem was not in my environment. The problem was in my heart. Both churches change lives. Both churches have phenomenal pastors. Both churches have broken people in them. The only difference is me and my ability to sit and listen to God. And while you may have a different career than I do, I know that if you're feeling unchallenged or unfulfilled in it, the first change necessary is to sit and listen to Jesus.

We had a man in The Rejuvenation Project that was unfulfilled in his career choice in the marketplace and believed he'd be better suited as a pastor. Our response to him was always the same: If you can't sit and listen in a marketplace job, then you can never sit and listen as a pastor. In fact, I would say that to everyone. If we don't sit and listen in our current circumstances, we won't sit and listen in our next ones, either. A change of circumstances or job will have a quick impact on our life and may help us feel better temporarily, but the long-term change will be fruitless if we can't sit and listen to God wherever we are.

I have heard a lot of well-meaning people pray a prayer, "God, I give you my 'Yes.' Take me where you want me to go and use me how you want to." I love the heart and hate the execution. I imagine God loves that prayer, but He has to think, "I would love to take you where I need you, but you don't even sit and listen to Me to know where I want you to go."

One time God woke me up at 3am every day for a week until I finally noticed it was Him. Once, I got out of bed and sat and listened, He spoke clear directions for my life. After hearing from God that night, I had to ask Him, "God, why did you have to wake me at 3am to tell me this?" His response was gentle and true. *That is the only time you'll listen.*

If we sit and listen and give glory to God in what we do, God will find us and take us where He needs us. Just ask Abraham, Moses, Daniel, Joseph, Mary, Noah, Peter, John, and the like. God used these people of God, but they had to sit and listen to God in some tough places before they ever received assurance or acclaim. Of all the people that understand the purpose of God, I think Paul and Silas know it best. They are witnessing all over the world for the Kingdom of God, but it's in a local jail at midnight that they find themselves living out their genuine purpose: praying and praising God (Acts 16:25).

It's God's job to change our circumstances. It is our job to give Him glory wherever we are. We have to sit and listen and obey. If we can master sitting and listening to God and then go where He leads us, we will never walk a day outside of His purpose for our life.

THE REJUVENATION PROJECT

First, ask the Holy Spirit what you will do in heaven. Write down what you believe he is telling you and then test it by asking yourself if this can be done today as well as in 10,000 years.

Next, let's identify what, in your life, is dirt and what is the breath of God. What part of your life is eternal and what part is just life? Pull out a piece of paper and revisit the last day or week. Make two columns. One column label "Dirt." Label the other "Breath of God." Work back through your day or week and put what you did in each column. Don't just look at the appearance of each activity. Look at the heart. For instance, attending church could go in either column depending on your attitude. If you went to church to give thanks to God in worship, put it in the "Breath of God" column. If you went out of duty and ended up gossiping with a friend afterwards, put that under "Dirt."

Ask yourself: "Which column takes more of my time?" Is there anything in the earthly impact column that you can turn into the eternal column by changing your attitude? Is there anything that needs to be on the list that isn't? Is there anything you want to remove from the list entirely?

Putting your life on paper is a great exercise for evaluating your life. The hope is to take almost everything that you do and turn it into the eternal column. You can do this, simply, by taking a heart posture of sitting with, listening to, and giving glory to God for everything He has done. It's not possible to completely remove the "dirt" from our life as long as we are on this earth living in a body of dust, but we should seek to turn as many hours as possible into the breath of God.

If you've worked through this chapter and still find yourself struggling because of what you do for a living, be intentional to sit and listen to the Father for a month. Most of the time, there will be a sense of relief to either move on and find a different career, school, or use of your time, or stick it out where you are. When God initiates change, go. When God asks you to stay put, stay. Don't be quick to assume God's opinion of your situation. Just sit. Just listen.

CHAPTER NINE

CHARACTER

OUR WORLD RISES and falls on leadership. With good leaders, we thrive. With bad leaders, we suffer. Our world needs good leaders, good parents, good teachers, and good coaches. What makes someone a good leader? Our world promotes good looks, charisma, wealth, and power, but in the Kingdom of Heaven, God spotlights character. Humans seem to spotlight everything *but* character. It's been said that character means doing the right thing even if nobody is watching. I think character also means doing the right thing even if *everybody* is watching. Do we always do the right thing? Probably not. So in this chapter, we'll learn how to grow in our character and opportunities for Kingdom promotion.

One of my mentors is one of the most dynamic Christian leaders I have ever met; a pastor that has been walking with God for over 50 years, preaching faithfully. His church has baptized thousands of people during his lifetime. He could retire today, but seems to be growing more passionate about advancing the Kingdom of God each day. In fact, the older he gets, the more and more enthused by the glorious gospel he seems to become. I asked him one day how he's able to live his last days on earth as his best days with Christ. What's the secret? He said two things: (1) character, and (2) purpose. We've already defined purpose in the last chapter, so let's focus on the definition of character now. "Character is how you walk faithfully in your life," he tells me. And when it comes to character, my mentor routinely says, "God will never promote someone beyond their character."

It sparks my curiosity that character is credited for faithfully walking with Christ for a lifetime. If we're interested in following Jesus passionately for just a decade of our life, let's just skip this section of the book. But if we're in this for the long haul, character is the insurance policy that will keep us from imploding. Do you want to have the integrity, humility, patience, joy, faithfulness, and self-control to make your last days on earth your best days? Read on.

Thomas Stanley wrote a book called *The Millionaire Mind.* He studied millionaires that earned more than $750,000 a year. By any standard, these are *really* rich people. The people surveyed were multimillionaires with an average net worth of over 9 million dollars. Stanley wanted to find the factors that caused these people to be wealthier than most. He didn't want to hear from just high-income earners, but rather the ones that have a high net worth *and* income. The results were surprising. The top factor noted by 733 of the people he studied wasn't a good childhood or an Ivy League degree or strong social connections. It was, simply, integrity - being honest with all people. "This measure of integrity... was tied for first in regard to the percentage of millionaires who rated it as a very important reason for their economic success," Stanley concludes. "If you lack integrity, most millionaires will tell you that you will not and should not graduate to economic success."[10]

Whatever our goal may be, whether riches on earth or riches in heaven, character is going to be a key building block for our maintained success. Character alone might not make us successful, but it will sustain whatever success we have. If we build on anything other than good character, we should expect failure. When we hear of disgraced leaders, what normally takes them down?

Typically, we call it a "moral failure." It's usually not a leadership failure. It's a *character* failure. Morals matter. Character matters.

The men and women that do the right thing no matter what are also the ones that firmly believe there are no moral exceptions. True character understands that we are no better than anyone else. We are all bent toward sin, and we are all tempted to lack integrity. Men and women of high integrity are aware that their own moral failure is just as much a possibility as the moral failings of everyone around them. The ones who say, *"I would never..."* or *"I don't understand how someone could..."* are dealing with pride, and pride ends in destruction. That prideful person may be successful on earth, but not by God's standards.

Paul says, "No temptation has overtaken you except what is common to mankind" (1 Corinthians 10:13, NIV). You are common. So am I. Your sin is common. So is mine. The only thing not common is our God, the ultimate giver of character. Good character can only come from true reliance on God, not from our efforts to become better or try harder. We are not naturally predisposed to good character. Nobody is the exception to sinful temptations. People that have high character are the ones who realize that the nature inside of them is not good, and keep their guard up to protect their lives.

In 1996, the United States Congress called upon the entertainment industry to establish a voluntary television rating system to provide parents with advance information on material that might be unsuitable for their children. The formation of this system is built on an assumption of maturity. While maturity is an important consideration for determining legal age requirements in driving, voting, employment or serving in the military, we have oddly adopted this same metric system for our entertainment. The rating "TV-MA," which stands for "Mature Audience Only" contains explicit sexuality, coarse language, and graphic violence. May I ask: is anybody - child or adult - mature enough to engage with such material and walk in righteousness? It's foolish to think such content would leave us unaffected. Friends, to lean on "maturity" as a validation for consuming sinful pleasures is prideful and will destroy our character. *There is no such thing as someone mature enough to handle sin and temptation.* If we don't want our kids engaging with that kind of material, we, too, must question our own consumption.

"Flee the evil desires of youth and pursue righteousness, faith, love and peace, along with those who call on the Lord out of a pure heart" (2 Timothy 2:22, NIV). Flee. Escape. Bolt. Do we hear the emphasis? We shouldn't dilly dally around people or things that have compromise written all over them. No one is strong enough to carry the weight of sin and temptation. If we understand our weakness, we have a shot at character. If we think we're stronger than the average person, beware.

I've never watched pornography. I don't drink alcohol and I don't gamble. You know why? I'd like it! I am so certain I would like these things, so I simply don't start. You may say, "Some of those things are okay in moderation." Maybe, but I don't trust myself that much. The best way to quit an addiction is to never start.

We have all known lives destroyed by each of these vices and others. My refusal of these practices isn't self-righteous as much as it is an acknowledgement of my humanness. We are all failure-prone. We are all weak in the face of addiction. No one dreams of being an addict of anything, but the road to addiction is paved with small compromises that are "no big deal" - until *they are.* When God calls us to flee, it means that we don't even want to be in the same zip code as these temptations. No one has the strength to stand before temptation day in and day out and remain firm in their character. Let's acknowledge our weakness by fleeing from as many temptations as we can possibly see and foresee.

"Indeed, there is no one on earth who is righteous, no one who does what is right and never sins" (Ecclesiastes 7:20, NIV). I hope I have made my point exceptionally clear. *The first step to high character is realizing you don't have it.* The only chance we have at character is to humbly acknowledge that we aren't good, and submit to the One who is.

Remember Chapter 1? We have to build our life on the foundation that God is good; that foundation is how we withstand life's storms. If we are not standing on the foundation of Christ's character, then our only hope is that it doesn't hurt too badly when we fall. We're not here to be hip, trendy Christian leaders. We are aiming for a lifetime of faithfulness to our God. And while we're all promised that, in this lifetime, we will have troubles, a solid character built on Christ can carry us through it all.

We cannot grow our character by our efforts alone. In fact, the less we are focused on ourselves the better. Our character grows to the level that we know Christ and His sufferings, and to the level we depend on the Holy Spirit. First, let's talk about Christ.

> In your relationships with one another, have the same mindset as Christ Jesus: Who, being in very nature God, did not consider equality with God something to be used to his own advantage; rather, he made himself nothing by taking the very nature of a servant, being made in human likeness. And being found in appearance as a man, he humbled himself by becoming obedient to death—even death on a cross! (Philippians 2:5-8, NIV)

To grow character suitable for the Kingdom of Heaven, our attitude must be the same as Christ Jesus. Even though He was God, He didn't rely on this power. Jesus knew He was no exception. Instead, He proved His ultimate character by being a servant. Jesus taught, "Anyone who wants to be first must be the very last, and the servant of all" (Mark 9:35, NIV). If we take the position of a willing, humble servant in any place we lead or function, our character will skyrocket.

"God opposes the proud, but shows favor to the humble" (James 4:6, NIV). Humility is evidence that we walk with Jesus because it is the very attitude that Christ carried when He was on earth. He humbled himself even to death on a cross. No one has served like Jesus. Shifting our eyes from ourselves and onto others will grow our character to the level of a Kingdom leader.

To briefly summarize: The first step to character is to realize we don't have it. The next step to character is to walk in the attitude of Jesus. The final step to producing good character is to seek out and depend on the Holy Spirit.

> But the fruit of the Spirit is love, joy, peace, forbearance, kindness, goodness, faithfulness, gentleness and self-control. Against such things there is no law." (Galatians 5:22-23, NIV)

The fruit of the Spirit is such a high level of character that there is no law that can come against it. But let me be clear: whose fruit is it? *Not yours!* It is "the fruit of the Spirit," not "the fruit of humans." If we exemplify the fruit of the Spirit, it isn't because we are special or well-bred or perfectly practiced in etiquette and esteem. It is, simply, because we are dependent on the Holy Spirit.

Similarly, if we feel we need to grow better in one of these qualities, it won't happen through grit or focus or the latest self-help bestseller, *Forbearance 101*. Rather, if we focus on acknowledging and obeying the Holy Spirit, we will not be deficient in any of these character qualities. Notice the word choice: "Fruit" in this passage is singular, not plural. We either have all of them or none of them. As much as we'd like, we cannot be 7 for 9 in the fruit of the Spirit. The fruit of the Spirit is pass/fail. If we notice a deficiency in *any* of these qualities, our goal is not to try harder and work on it alone, our goal is to become more aware of the Holy Spirit. He is the source. He is the grower and giver of fruit.

One of my favorite questions to ask people is "What is God teaching you right now?" I love to ask it because I find it so cool to see how God intricately works in all of our lives. However, I've noticed a pattern in the answers of most people. If someone doesn't know what God is teaching them, they'll spout off whatever they feel deficient in. Take patience, for example. The reason why so many of us rarely feel patient is because we try to grow our own patience. To become fully patient though requires the work of the Holy Spirit, not us.

If we want to grow in any quality like self-control, patience, love or kindness, but we are not regularly sitting with, listening to, and worshiping the Holy Spirit, then we will never attain the fruit of the Spirit in our lives. I don't believe God is teaching us things like patience or self-control as much as we think. The Holy Spirit knows these things are not to be taught as much as they are to be *received*. I believe He would much rather give us a bigger revelation of Jesus Christ then watch us loath another attempt to acquire good character by our own works.

In our American churches, we love to plan Bible studies and Sunday morning sermons on specific topics so that we might acquire them. I respect the desire, but hate the implementation. Whether the study centers on purity, love, patience, or all manner of Christian principles, the reality is this: there is something better to focus on that will take care of it all. The more we sit and think about the Father, Jesus, and the Holy Spirit, the more we will receive all blessings and more importantly *character*. Jesus counsels us to turn from our worries and deficiencies and instead "seek first his kingdom and his righteousness, and all these things will be given to you as well" (Matthew 6:33, NIV). The road to solid character is as narrow as the road to eternal life. We will only get there through Jesus.

HOW IS YOUR CHARACTER TODAY?

The fastest way to judge our character - and someone else's - is through the mouth. Character is a heart issue, but out of the overflow of the heart, the mouth speaks (Luke 6:45). If we want to see where our character is, let's pay attention to what we talk about. If we have a bent toward gossip, slander, crude talk, sarcasm, and bitterness, then we are likely dealing with character issues that could stem from a variety of places.

As a youth pastor, one of the most beneficial periods of ministry I have experienced thus far was centered around high school boys as we focused on becoming men of our word. The challenge was simple: whatever we said we were going to do, *we had to do it.* We were done being wishy-washy and full of just good intentions. One particular evening, we each committed aloud to following through with something specific in the coming week. Nothing too crazy; we set the bar low. I didn't want these young men to be the men that had big dreams and small follow-through. What if we started with small dreams and big follow-through?

At first, we began with an unspiritual commitment. One boy said, "I commit to eating a turkey sandwich for lunch every day for a week." Do you know what? This simple commitment changed his life. He learned to follow through and be a man of his word - not just in lunch, but in all things. He faithfully follows Christ, and has since lost almost 100 lbs. by being a man of his word. Eating a turkey sandwich didn't change his life. His growing *character* changed his life and it evidenced in his words and follow-through.

If we desire our character to improve, we will need our words to improve. Simply trying to maintain self-control with our tongue will not suffice. We don't get character from our efforts, we get them from Christ's. Therefore, we must remain faithful to many of the lessons we have already covered.

A quick review of The Rejuvenation Project's central tenets: be washed by the Word, listen to the Holy Spirit, and walk in forgiveness. To truly walk in these three principles, God must be our central focal point. This is what breeds our character. Thus, character is more of a byproduct of our walk with God than it is a goal to be achieved.

God has made us to lead and live a powerful life on this earth. Humans will promote for any reason, but God will promote us to the level of our character. It is my hope that we all desire Kingdom promotion more than worldly promotion. If you want to grow your character, I urge you, don't try harder. Humble yourself, replicate the attitude of Jesus, and daily acknowledge the heart of the Holy Spirit. For in this, you will never be deficient in any good thing.

THE REJUVENATION PROJECT

Note: *The Rejuvenation Project exercise for this chapter will take time to bear fruit. I implore you to not give up. Remember: your current life is a product of your actions and habits from six months ago.*

Imagine I challenged you to walk around with a 16oz cup of water in your hand for a day and that I would give you $1,000 for every ounce of water the cup still held at the end of the day. You'd live your life differently, wouldn't you? You would *always* be focused on that cup of water in your hand. You'd try desperately not to spill anything.

For this exercise, I want you to take that same obsessive mindset and apply it to the Holy Spirit. The Holy Spirit will teach you about Jesus' attitude and will produce the fruit of the Spirit in your life. If you want to start to grow in character, you must start with obsessive attention to the Spirit. Be aware of the Spirit in every move you make. So, simply, *your job is to think about the Holy Spirit as much as you can in a day.*

Thinking about the Holy Spirit won't come naturally; you must train for it. Start by setting a reminder on your phone for every hour or two. Begin to think about Him at this reminder. Maybe you could also habit stack Holy Spirit thinking onto something you already do regularly, like eating or brushing your teeth. If you drive a lot, consider turning off the radio and thinking about Him in silence. If I was given a challenge to carry a cup of water and I didn't want to spill it, you know what I would do for most of that day? I would move less. I would sit more. Just as motion can cause water to spill, motion can also decrease our ability to think about the Holy Spirit. No, I am not telling you to be a monk and never move, nor to become a certified couch potato. But what we carry - and how we carry it - matters.

Can you walk slower? Can you pull out our phone only when you need it? Can you direct your steps and your days with intention? Your life pace and focus reflect the value you place on the Holy Spirit. Scripture never emphasized a fast-paced life. If you are simply too busy or distracted to think about the Holy Spirit, you have two options: change your pace, or wait for a moral failure. Seek after God and His righteousness and all the rest will fall into place.

A loving disclaimer: Don't tell yourself this doesn't work until you have practiced faithfully for six months. A lot of us are good at doing things for three weeks. If we only focus on the Holy Spirit for three weeks, we will not see character change. The timeline on seeing this fruit will be about six months. Don't give up!

Throughout this exercise, watch your words. Your character flows from your mouth. If you wouldn't say it from the pulpit, reconsider it. You may find that you do really well thinking about the Holy Spirit - that is - until your toddler wakes up grouchy or you have that staff meeting you were dreading. In the moments you find yourself speaking something that wouldn't be the character of Christ, repent as quickly as you can. Pray something like, "Holy Spirit, what I said was wrong. I'm sorry. Please keep growing my character to be like Jesus."

Finally, Flee! What, in your world, is routinely tempting you? Don't tolerate sin and compromise around you. Yes, be radical. Be weird. Others may think your boundaries and personal convictions are overkill, but you don't want to be promoted by your peers, you want to be promoted by your God. Run like Joseph out of Potiphar's house (Genesis 39). If you do not flee, you might stand firm for years, but not a lifetime. Temptation is like waves at the beach: Each one feels insignificant, but a lifetime of them will erode a shoreline until it falls in the ocean. Temptation will creep in quietly and consistently until we fall into it. Friend, it's time to get off the beach.

CHAPTER TEN

THE SPARK TO BURNOUT

CHANCES ARE, WE are all familiar with the feeling of burnout. Our experiences of burnout could be minor, like being burnt out on certain food we eat or a movie our kids watch three times a day. Or, our experience of burnout could feel earth-shattering, like when we grow tired of our family, our job, our marriage, or ultimately our God. Whether small or great, burnout doesn't happen overnight. We don't just wake up one morning, shocked by the fact that our life isn't working the way it used to. The reality is that burnout is a slow burn that begins from the tiniest of sparks. So, instead of focusing solely on how to recuperate *from* burnout, let's spend time exploring what guides us *to* burnout. Most major forest fires can be traced back to a small spark. Similarly, there is one spark that leads to burnout every single time. *That spark is called control.*

No one likes to feel like their life is spinning out of control. I think we all want peace and tranquility of heart. But the method by which we try to achieve a life of order makes all the difference in whether or not we ultimately receive it. While the logical step to gaining control is to begin managing every situation and person around us, this always backfires. Why? Because, in more cases than not, the more we try to control what goes on in our life, the more out of control it will become.

Control often masks itself behind the belief that *what goes on outside of us determines what is inside of us.* We work to manipulate our environments in order to make us feel good inside. In God's economy, the reverse is required: *What is inside of us always impacts what is outside of us.*

Years ago, after welcoming a seasoned pastor into The Rejuvenation Project I asked him what he wished he had known when he first began in ministry. His response was simple: "I wish I would have known that being a pastor wouldn't fix my issues." This pastor believed the way to fix himself was to control his circumstances; a method that caused years of unnecessary pain. So many of us believe that if we can change our circumstances, we can change our life. But changing our circumstances is like putting a band-aid on a gunshot wound. It may stop the bleeding, but the bullet's still there. If we want our life to change, we have to dig deeper below the surface.

When I run into someone who is struggling with any issue in life, I've noticed that, initially, they describe their issue by offering details about what is going on in their outward circumstances; relational issues, health issues, work issues, etc. We assume these outward problems all have many outward solutions, right? Instead, there is often just one solution, and it can only be found within us: *surrender.*

How rarely we seek this solution. How rarely we pray for true submission to the will of God. We pray a lot of prayers for God to intervene in our lives. We love to tell God what we need Him to do to make everything better, for us to look and feel our best. But God cares more about what is *inside* of us.

Let me be as clear as possible: If God isn't answering our prayers the way we anticipate, He probably doesn't think our solution is a good idea. He knows more than we do. How many times have we wrongly assumed God didn't answer our prayer, when truly, our prayer was just us trying to control God? How many times do we use prayer to offer our human solutions to heart problems, like some sort of cosmic suggestion box? Our prayer should not be, "God, I don't like my circumstances. Are there any you want to change?" The prayers that God really loves to answer are, "God, I don't like my circumstances. Is there anything in my heart or mind that you want to change?"

To be clear, a change of circumstance can certainly be helpful. But a change in circumstance should always follow or accompany a change of heart. Let's not clamor for control of our outside world just to make peace with our inward struggles. Rather, we should make peace with the fact that our life belongs to God and He is in control of our world. Then, and only then, can we be moved by the Spirit into His ultimate plans for our life. We cannot let the wind of the Spirit move us if we are tied down by our own power and choice.

When my wife and I were just a few years into marriage, things were not going well. In fact, our relationship was the worst it had ever been. There wasn't anything immoral between us, but the discontent we both experienced was sky high. Together, we decided that we should move to a new city and start over. We really felt God leading this move, but we also understood that simply moving wouldn't change anything. We'd still be us, just in a different zip code.

So, in the four months leading up to our move, we sought out healing. Ironically, all of the healing that needed to take place had nothing to do with our address and had everything to do with our hearts. Changing and surrendering our inner lives and then changing our outward lives based on the guidance from God was the recipe for success. The key though was surrendering our control. We were done manipulating our lives to our own selfish interests. Once we did that, God could move us as He wished.

Control is a lordship issue. We want Jesus to save us from our sins, but in reality, we still want to be our own Lord. When we give our life to Jesus, who then has our life? Jesus. We gave it to Him. It is no longer in our possession or control. Salvation and control are polar opposites. The very essence of needing saved screams, "Help! I don't have control!"

My dad always taught me that we can have intimacy or we can have control, but we cannot have both. Deep down, we all crave intimacy with God, our family, and our friends. When those relationships are stretched, we have a choice: Do we try to control the actions of others so we can feel short-term peace, or do we surrender control to experience long-term connection? Control steals intimacy which steals connection, leaving us lonely and untethered: a direct path to burnout.

The reason our love of control burns us so deeply is because our perspective is so limited. We think we know best, but we don't. God leads us in the way we should go with eyes that can see both ends of eternity. I lead myself based on what I am feeling in a moment. Who do we think has a better grip on reality? Remember, there is a way that seems right and, in the end, it leads to death (Proverbs 14:12).

My grandparents have been alive about 90 years and today are living as close to the Lord as ever. To me, they are the model for living our last days as our best days with Christ. But if you asked them, they wouldn't say their current circumstances are the best circumstances of their life. In fact, on their 60th wedding anniversary, they were asked what the hardest part of marriage was, and both of my grandparents responded, "Right now." Despite tough trials or declining health, their love for the Lord hasn't wavered. In fact, the older my grandpa gets, the more his advice simplifies. When I see him now, he will only tell me how wonderful it is to be surrendered to God and that He is in control. Oh, how sweet it is to trust in Jesus.

Resting in the sovereignty of God means slowly releasing the grip of our own free will. When we choose to give our life to Jesus, we take our first step into the sovereign plan of God. As we surrender more to God as our life continues, we are taking one more step into God's sovereignty. Thus, the promise of Proverbs 3:5-6 comes alive "Trust in the Lord with all your heart and lean not on your own understanding; in all your ways submit to him, and he will make your paths straight" (NIV). Without multiple moments of submission throughout our lives, we will never be able to walk on the straight path God makes for us.

Many mentors of mine echo this same sentiment: the older they get, the less they feel in control. Why? Because they have pursued a lifetime of surrender to God. When they were young, they felt their faith moved heaven and earth, but now they know God will simply do whatever He wants with their lives because He has control. In the same way, we each begin our lives full of free will. But I hope we don't stay there. My desire is that we will slowly come to the end of our lives in full pursuit of the sovereignty of God by surrendering the entirety of our free will to Him. Every day, I want to surrender a little bit more so that He can do whatever He wants with me.

Our level of rejuvenation is directly tied to our level of surrender. To say it another way: *The less we control, the less likely we are to burn out.* Why do marriages end? Control. Why do children disobey? Control. Why is there injustice in the world? Control. What makes people addicted to substances? Control. More specifically, most of the struggles that lead us away from a rejuvenated life revolve around *who is in control of our life.* If we are in control, then it is our responsibility to make our nonprofit run well, even at the expense of our family. If we are in control, we will need to experience a lot of guilt and shame for our sins before we feel punished enough to move on. If we are in control, we will never experience true rest or lasting abundance. We will grow weaker and more tired by the day. If we keep playing with the spark of control, we will certainly burn with it.

The human mind believes that if you don't like your life, you should change your circumstances. The Kingdom of God says, if you don't like your life, give it up. "Look to the Lord and His strength; seek His face always" (Psalm 105:4, NIV). Notice the verse doesn't say "Look to the Lord and His strength, so that He does whatever *you* think is best." We are to look to the Lord and His strength, which will assure our hearts that He is in control. Our response is to *keep seeking him.*

When I was younger, God gave me specific directions to follow for the entirety of my life. At first, I didn't know if these steps were just my idea or if this was God's voice. But the older I get, the more I know it was Him:

Step 1: Put God first.
Step 2: Seek His face.
Step 3: Do what is right.

As a young man, I wrote these steps on a piece of paper, and looking at Step 3, thought, "How am I supposed to know what the right thing to do is?"

I realize now, over a decade later, that there is a reason step 3 is step 3. If I put God first in all things and seek His face, then I will do what is right. In other words, completing step 1 and 2 naturally leads to the accomplishment of step 3. The reason so many of us burn out is because we jump straight to the third step. We believe the lie that doing the right thing will get us closer to God. We run around trying to figure out what is the right way to live while disregarding the fact that making God first in everything *is* the right way to live. On earth, we are judged by whether or not we did the right thing. In heaven, we are judged by whether or not Jesus knows us. If we take care of step 1 and 2 then God will lead us to step 3.

NOT BY WORKS... TO DO GOOD WORKS

Our works won't save us. "For it is by grace you have been saved, through faith—and this is not from yourselves, it is the gift of God—not by works, so that no one can boast" (Ephesians 2:8-9, NIV). I don't meet many Christians that have a problem with those two verses, but I do see a lot of people get burnt out by what they think the following verse means: "For we are God's handiwork, created in Christ Jesus to do good works, which God prepared in advance for us to do" (Ephesians 2:10, NIV). Many of us read this and think, "I am saved by Jesus and I must work hard to do what He says so that I pay him back with my good works." We understand that we aren't saved by our actions, but when we read our call to do good works, we pile on the pressure anyway.

At first glance, these verses seem to be in complete contradiction to each other, but they're not. We are saved by grace, and then, we work *from that same grace.* We are made to do good works, but those good works are not in our control or timing. They are prepared by God; therefore, they belong to Him. That's why our spiritual nudges don't always make sense, or often lack convenience. They're God's, not ours.

Once, I went to a local hardware store to get some supplies for a house project I was working on. I wasn't thinking about Christ or anything spiritual, just that the store would be closing in an hour and I wanted to be sure I had enough time to purchase everything I needed. As I pulled into my parking spot, I had a distinct thought from the Holy Spirit: *I got someone in there for you.* I'll be honest, I don't get too excited when the Holy Spirit tells me this stuff. In fact, I often dread it. I tried to reason that it was just my thoughts, but I have become too aware of God's voice to disregard the nudge to do His work.

As I walked into the hardware store, I immediately started looking at people and thinking, "Is that the person I need to talk to? Maybe him? Or is it her?" I realize now why I dread when God asks me to do something. As soon as I get His prompting, I immediately take full control on the follow-through. I get frustrated because God didn't give me more directions, and I ultimately feel like I fail Him more than I actually do what He wants.

About three minutes into navigating a big store trying to figure out who the Holy Spirit had in there for me, I could feel my anxiety and frustrations mounting. I knew what I had to do: I had to surrender. I needed to surrender control of God's good works for me. It was undeniable that God had someone in there for me, but I was working in my own power to make it happen. So I prayed, "God, you said you have someone in here for me, and I can't figure this out on my own. I am going to grab what I came for and if you bring the person to me or myself to them, I will talk to them." As soon as I prayed this, the anxiety left. How many times has my response to the Holy Spirit's prompting unconsciously been, "Great! Thanks for the information. I will take it from here, God"? But God doesn't tell us what to do so we can prove our worth. He tells us so He can prove Himself faithful.

When I found everything I needed inside the store and reached the checkout lane, a young lady began to share with me about her health problems, which led to struggles with her life. She opened up completely after only a simple, everyday, common courtesy question from me: "How's your day going?" After listening for a few minutes, I said, "May I pray for you to be healed?" She said, "Sure, but I doubt anything will happen." I prayed with her and walked out. I don't know what happened to her, but I do know that it is God's job to work it out.

As I walked toward the parking lot, I felt such a sense of peace. I did what God asked me to do, and because I let Him have control over the process and the outcome, it was easy. Even in the good works God prepares for us, we must surrender. I implore every reader: Give up control of your life and you will extinguish the first and most scorching spark to burnout.

FREE FROM ANXIETY

Our culture talks openly and easily about anxiety, and nearly everyone I know has experienced some form of it. While some experience severe cases that require medication, others experience anxiety not as a result of imbalanced chemicals, but imbalanced control.

When I was in middle school, I spent an entire summer struggling with anxiety. I didn't want to be away from my parents and eventually I never wanted to leave the house. I was consistently overwhelmed everywhere I went. One night, I finally mustered up the courage to tell my dad how I was feeling. The conversation was short, but I still remember his response: "It sounds like you need to surrender to Jesus." We prayed for Jesus to be in control of my life. I have never felt that level of anxiety again. Sometimes, when I can feel it start to creep back into my life, I put that fire out before it starts by repeating to myself that *Jesus is in control of my life and I am not.*

Surrendering control is not something that happens once. As life progresses, deeper levels of surrender are required from us. When we give our life to the Lord for the first time, we assume we are giving all of our life to Him. But truly, we're probably giving just a small portion. We may only have rightful ownership of 25% of our life because we have given the other 75% over to other idols: hobbies, dreams, work, places, people, money, addictions, social media or even food. The list of idols is endless. Similarly, how could I truly surrender my marriage or children when I gave my life to Jesus first as 6th grader. Some things can not be surrendered at first because God has yet to give them to us. Regardless of why we can't surrender all to God at first, He takes our first offering knowing it's not everything, and over time, He will gently and graciously call for more.

Whenever I sense the Holy Spirit showing me another object or area of my life I must surrender, I will initially be sad or full of pride, but then I remind myself that God doesn't take stuff to be mean; He takes stuff so He can give us more of Himself. So, if you find yourself questioning why - or what - God's calling you to surrender, take heart: there's another part of your life God is seeking to rejuvenate.

THE REJUVENATION PROJECT

It's one thing to read about surrendering control; it's another thing to actually give it up. The freedom of Christ will come through the practice of dethroning yourself as the lord of your life, and crowning Jesus instead. Chances are, the Spirit of God has brought something specific to the forefront of your mind as you read this very chapter. If so, just go ahead and stop here and take the action that you feel is necessary. If you don't yet have an idea of what area of life you need to give up control in, explore the below guiding questions:

1. What is a problem you are dealing with in your own life?

    a. What steps have you taken in your own power to fix that problem?
    b. Now give that problem and all of your solutions to God.

2. What is a problem in someone else's life close to you?

    a. What steps have you taken to try to fix them or their problem in your own power?
    b. Now give that person, problem and your solutions to God.

If you have worked through those two prompts and haven't discovered anything you're trying to control in your life, I suggest you seek the counsel of those closest to you. They will probably be able to give you a substantial list.

The practice of surrendering control is an ongoing process. It's like mowing the lawn: without regular maintenance, it quickly grows out of hand. The human spirit loves control. Our desire to micromanage every detail will grow back quietly at first, but stay diligent as you continue to surrender. Slowly but surely, your tendency to control will begin to diminish.

Lastly, never assume you are completely surrendered. Always be on guard and quick to repent when you seem to be taking charge over God. Below are some prayers you can regularly pray to maintain a posture that gives rightful control to the lordship of Jesus Christ:

> "Jesus, I surrender trying to control my parents. They are not mine, but Yours."

> "Jesus, I surrender trying to control my children. They are not mine, but Yours."

> "Jesus, I surrender trying to control my spouse. They are

not mine, but Yours."

"Jesus, I surrender trying to control my job. It is not mine, but Yours."

"Jesus, I surrender trying to control your church. It is not mine, but Yours."

"Jesus, I surrender trying to control my money. It is not mine, but Yours."

"Jesus, I surrender trying to control my schedule. It is not mine, but Yours."

"Jesus, I surrender trying to control my body. It is not mine, but Yours."

"Jesus, I surrender trying to control ________. All is Yours!"

CHAPTER ELEVEN

THE HEAVENLY PACE

AS A PASTOR, I've had to learn a lot of things, one of which is the fine art of small talk. On any given Sunday morning, I might engage in dozens of 45-second conversations. As I've become more fluent in the art of quick conversing, I've started to notice a pattern in the conversations I share with others. When I ask how someone is doing, often they'll respond, "Oh I am good, just busy!" I've said it. You've said it. We've all said it. But when did "good" and "busy" become synonyms? We're so quick to spotlight how busy we are, like it's the badge of honor. After all, if we aren't drowning in work or family commitments, are we even a good person?

There are many great books written on the subject of resting, slowing down, and being addicted to hurrying. So many, in fact, that I think we should make any book on this topic a part of our regular reading cycles just as a reminder to slow down when busyness tries to creep into our lives. But for our purposes, let's explore the topic of busyness as it relates to (or, more aptly, *doesn't*) the heart posture of The Rejuvenated Life. If we're chronically busy, we're probably not living a rejuvenated life. And while the world will offer us thousands of tips to become a better organizer of our schedule, the answer lies far beyond the calendar. Busyness isn't a time management issue; it's a heart issue.

Let's start with the concept of *pace*. Pacing is a major theme of The Rejuvenated Life because we are aiming to have our last days be our best days, which requires endurance. When we pace ourselves, we conserve our energy now so that we have more energy later. It's not just a physical concept; it's a spiritual one, too. Paul defines our spiritual lives as running a race. "Do you not know that in a race all the runners run, but only one gets the prize? Run in such a way as to get the prize" (1 Corinthians 9:24, NIV). What's the goal? Win the prize. We don't want to run too quickly only to find ourselves losing in the end. Remember the tortoise and the hare? Slow and steady wins the race. No one is applauded in heaven by how they start the race, but rather, by how they finish.

To win our race, we have to run at a *heavenly pace*. Heavenly pace seeks to honor God's original design for the rhythms of humanity - work and rest. To say that the work of the Kingdom of Heaven involves nothing but sitting is a misnomer, and to say that the Kingdom of Heaven revolves around how much work we get done is an insult to God's power and character. We want to walk at a heavenly pace, the pace set at the dawn of time. But what is it?

"Six days you shall labor, but on the seventh day you shall rest; even during the plowing season and harvest you must rest" (Exodus 34:21, NIV). In the Bible, the number seven is a number representing wholeness or perfection. To live in the fullness of God, we have to be fluent at working *and* resting. We cannot get to wholeness by just working and we cannot get to wholeness by just resting. We're going to need both. 6 + 1 = 7. This is the only equation to get to the perfect pace in life.

The good news is this: Work and rest are designed to work beautifully together. We have to work to rest and we have to rest to work. But it's important to note which comes first. When we read the account of creation in Genesis 1, there is a common phrase used to signal the completion of days. It reads, "And there was evening, and there was morning." The order here is significant.

In our modern world, we start each day in the morning. In Hebrew culture, the day began in the evening. Why is this significant? God realizes that the first priority in each day is to rest. In our minds, we start each day by waking up. We see how much we can cram into a day, and with whatever time is left, we sleep. But to God, going to sleep is the priority. It's the first thing we do each day. God has designed our day to begin with rest. Only then can we work from a place of rest, rather than resting from a place of exhaustion. This is huge! Resting first emphasizes our trust in God. Resting first is like giving God a head start on the work He has placed before us.

Let's imagine we spent ten minutes each evening asking God what He wants from us for the day. Once we feel some direction of what God would have us do, the next action we take is to crawl under the covers and sleep. That sounds wild, right? But it's precisely by God's design. The very act of rest recognizes that God will go before us and work on our behalf. I'd even surmise that we'll get more accomplished when we *start* with rest rather than finish with it. This sort of practice feels a lot like the offering of first fruits. God doesn't like seconds. He wants our firsts.

We shouldn't rest *after* our work is done, but rather before we begin. God wishes to be with us *in* our work. He goes before us and behind us. Changing the orientation of our days to reflect that truth might actually be the most productive and restful thing we could ever do.

Once, I was in the middle of a particularly busy season at my church. I had loads of planning and studying to complete for an upcoming retreat. It was Monday, and I already felt overwhelmed and behind on my work. I decided I should just buckle down, power through, and get the work done. But something was off in my spirit. So I paused, and I prayed.

I felt God nudge me to go sit with Him at a park for the afternoon. On one hand, this sounded absurd. I had a full week ahead, and I already felt the weight of busyness on me. But on the other hand, I felt a stronger weight, a request from God telling me to leave it behind and be with Him. The decision was an obvious one.

Normally, I like to spend time with God after I get my work done, so I have less distractions. But this time, I was going to spend time with God *in* all the distractions. Even though I kept hearing the voice of fear tell me that if I gave up an afternoon, my work wouldn't get completed, I left my office and went to the park. I sat with God for an hour or so. No big revelations occurred. After I was done, instead of going back to church, I sensed the Spirit telling me to go home to my family. So I did. Again, no big revelations. I trusted God, but in the back of my mind, I knew I still had all my work to do.

I used to think God was somehow opposed to our work, as if our to-do list was in direct competition with our time alone with Him. But I am now aware that God is not opposed to our work. Instead, He desires to participate in completing it. That week, after giving up an afternoon on the front end, every bit of my work was completed, and I had enough time left over to enjoy a free afternoon on the last day of the work week. It wasn't that I overestimated how much my workload was; it was that I underestimated how much God would partner with me in accomplishing it. That whole week, other people filled gaps. My brain was sharp. The sermons I wrote felt downloaded into my brain. I felt a renewed ease, a heightened focus, and an immersive flow within my work. It was all abundantly clear: God was working with me!

God can do more in a second than we can do in a lifetime, yet, all too often, we don't depend on Him to help us work. We pray for provision, but why don't we ever ask God where our next sales call should be or how to build better systems? God wants to be involved in our work; He's just waiting for a promotion. The model of working and resting was first established by God himself. He worked *and* rested, and He wants to partner with us in both. In other words, we don't have to keep doing it alone! We must embrace the heavenly pace.

SABBATH

It is becoming increasingly difficult to recognize truth from lies in our world, especially amongst our Christian communities. How do we know if someone is truly submitted to the will of God? There is no shortage of people that claim Jesus as Lord, but how do we know we can trust what they say? It's not as difficult as we think. The defining feature of the closest and most dynamic of Jesus' followers is, surprisingly, *rest*. A devoted follower of Christ will have a life marked by rest, specifically a Sabbath. How do we know if someone is truly a disciple of Jesus? It's not miracles or prophecy or even evangelism. Those that walk with the Lord will honor the Sabbath.

Let me clarify: Sabbath is not just a day off. A day off, for most of us, is taking a day off from the work we get paid to do so we can do the work we do *not* get paid to do, like chores, errands, or appointments But a Sabbath is a day absent from *all ordinary work*. As Christians, we are commanded to work for six days, and on the seventh day, we are to rest.

I used to think that a Sabbath day was part of the old covenant, more of a suggestion than a rule of life. Then I read the ten commandments in Exodus 20 and recognized that, even though those commandments were given before Jesus established the new covenant, they are still pertinent today. Even now, as I read through the list of ten commandments, I recognize that I still adhere faithfully to nine out of the ten. Most of us believe murder, lying, adultery, worshiping idols, or placing anything before God is wrong. We still believe honoring parents is the right way to live. But then, we encounter commandment number four:

> Remember the Sabbath day by keeping it holy. Six days you shall labor and do all your work, but the seventh day is a sabbath to the LORD your God. On it you shall not do any work, neither you, nor your son or daughter, nor your male or female servant, nor your animals, nor any foreigner residing in your towns. For in six days the LORD made the heavens and the earth, the sea, and all that is in them, but he rested on the seventh day. Therefore the LORD blessed the Sabbath day and made it holy. (Exodus

20:8-11, NIV)

Let's be honest; this commandment is a lot less accepted today. While I am not suggesting that our world is perfectly faithful to every other commandment, I do have a concern that so many of God's people have no conviction for this command compared to the others. After all, most of the people who commit adultery know, on some inherent level, it is wrong. Not so with the Sabbath. Mostly, we ignore it. Few feel any remorse over it. Even fewer practice it, setting aside a day each week to call holy. I believe this is one of the greatest deceptions the enemy has working against the Church in our time. Is the Sabbath just a part of the old covenant law that no longer pertains to us? Let's reconsider.

In Ezekiel 20, the prophet Ezekiel speaks on behalf of the Lord against Israel. More specifically, God is punishing Israel because they rejected the laws He established *and* they desecrated His Sabbaths. Six times in Ezekiel 20, the Word of the Lord highlights a distinction between the law and the Sabbath. This should pique our curiosity, because our God doesn't associate the Sabbath as a law. Rather, it's a gift.

Whereas laws may feel constricting to humanity, Jesus makes a clear statement that the Sabbath is a gift given to us. "Then he said to them, 'The Sabbath was made for man, not man for the Sabbath'" (Mark 2:27, NIV). And yet, somewhere along the line, we started to view it as a punishment. For many, the teaching of Sabbath doesn't provoke joy, but actually a sense of dread. Why? Because we live in a 24/7 culture that testifies we can work harder, go faster, and know better than God. Friends, this is not the testimony I want to be giving (nor living). The Lord has established that we are not to live 24/7, but 24/6. Remember: 6 + 1 = completeness. We are to set aside one day, each and every week, as holy.

Many of us remember that the Israelites walked away from God in many ways and were exiled in Babylon for 70 years. But few of us understand the significance of that timeline. Why 70 years? Well, for approximately 490 years, God's command to leave the land unplowed and unused every seven years was ignored. The

Israelites hadn't been giving the land rest, and now the land was truly going to get the rest it required (See 2 Chronicles 36:21, Leviticus 26:34-35). God's rest will never be circumvented. It's better to adhere to the heavenly pace than to be pushed aside by God to make room for rest.

Hebrews 4 makes it incredibly clear: "Therefore, since the promise of entering his rest still stands, let us be careful that none of you be found to have fallen short of it" (v. 1, NIV). "There remains, then, a Sabbath-rest for the people of God; for anyone who enters God's rest also rests from their works, just as God did from his" (v. 9-10, NIV). The Sabbath remains for all time.

Here, then, is why Sabbath is the defining outward physical feature of a true disciple of Jesus. We are saved by grace, not by works. Without a weekly rhythm that helps us remember this beautiful truth - that we are saved not by what we do - we will drift further and further from the grace that we experienced when we first believed. The Sabbath is a tactile testimony of the grace of God. If we are not marked by the grace found through the blood of Jesus, we are not in Christ. Grace is a big deal! Therefore, we should do everything the Lord established to help us remember this grace.

The person who commits to work on a day set aside to remember that we do not exist by our own commitment to work will experience confusion and hypocrisy. The person who ignores the gift of Sabbath will have an immensely difficult time connecting the truth of God's grace between their head and their heart. The person who sits in a Sunday service and hears the message of grace while mentally preparing a long list of things to be accomplished as soon as service ends will be unable to truly comprehend that we are saved by grace and not by works.

We must regularly pause to let the grace of God penetrate our hearts. Otherwise, all we have is head knowledge that is left unaccompanied by belief and practice. The grace of God isn't only available for a once-in-a-lifetime prayer of salvation. The grace of God is to be evidenced once a week, lived as a patterned reminder in remembrance of that gift. We Sabbath because Jesus saved us on the cross, and His grace was - and still is - unearned. May we be marked by that truth in every area of our life.

STRATEGIES FOR THE HEAVENLY PACE

One of the biggest challenges to the heavenly pace is the voice in our heads saying, "More!" Walking in the heavenly pace is not about how we start things, but rather how we end. This is true about the race of life, but also true about each individual task or project we are working on. We read in Colossians 3 that we are to work as if we are serving the Lord, not man. Therefore, many Christians live by a mantra of excellence in the name of the Lord Jesus. While I certainly believe in seeking excellence, the process can become destructive if we assume excellence is just another word for *more*.

Let's consider a sermon, a homework assignment, or a presentation you are preparing for. At what point is it good enough? I have found great insight in Craig Groeschel's teaching called GETMO: Good Enough to Move On. Here's the gist: If I spend two hours working on a sermon, I will have a sermon. If I spend seven hours on that sermon, I will have a much better sermon. The extra time I spend on that sermon will dramatically increase the quality of the sermon. Therefore, you and I would likely find it acceptable to devote even more time to my sermon since it will only grow in quality, right?

But let's say I spend thirty hours on the sermon. I will now have spent over four times the amount of time I'd spent on the previous draft, and fifteen times more hours than the original. So, will my new sermon be four times better than the seven-hour sermon? Probably not. More is not always better. Pastor Groeschel says it like this, "Over time, investing more always brings a diminishing return. Look for the greatest level of return based on time, money, and resources invested."[11] Once we find the sweet spot - the best quality for the right investment of time - move on!

Pastor Groeschel is aware that one of the quickest shortcuts to burnout is when we can't - or don't know when to - say, "Enough!"

Proverbs 30:15-16 says "The leech has two suckers that cry out, "More, more!" There are three things that are never satisfied—no, four that never say, "Enough!": the grave, the barren womb, the thirsty desert, the blazing fire" (NLT). Scripture understands that this world has a never ending desire for more. It cannot be satisfied. GETMO is such an important strategy for implementing heavenly pace because it helps us live with the end in mind, whether we're applying the principle to something as simple as a twenty-minute sermon or as profound as a career change. If we don't stand up and declare enough is enough, we will become dead and dry in the quest for more.

Friends, there is nothing that we can physically do that God is not capable of doing Himself. He is gracious to include us in His work. When we work, we work to serve the voice of the Spirit of God, not the voice in our head screaming, "More!" We serve a God who whispers. Often, He will say, "Move on." before He says, "More!"

Now, let's address some Sabbath strategies. There is a simple phrase I repeat on the day of Sabbath that helps me set a proper pace without rigid rules or complicated boundaries: *No striving.* We are not saved by what we do; therefore, a true Sabbath is one where we do not seek to advance our lives. In our technological world, the line between work and rest is exceptionally blurry. The Pharisees were once mad at Jesus because His disciples picked grain in a field on the Sabbath (Mark 2:23-28), an activity clearly related to work. After all, nobody rests in a labor field! But for us, our work and life are so intertwined with technology that it can often be hard to determine when we are working or resting. We need to firm up the line, not so we become a Pharisee, but so we can live in the grace of God.

The Sabbath is not a day that can be achieved, but rather received. Therefore, we mustn't make a list of activities that are or are not acceptable on a Sabbath day. This rigidity would turn Sabbath into a religious activity more than a gift from God. However, there are some principles that can help us establish a restful pace for our households.

A Sabbath day must look vastly different than the other six days. If we barely notice a difference in the day we set apart versus the other six, we are not making it holy. The way I determine what I should or shouldn't do on a Sabbath is that any activity that tries to better my standing in life is off limits on the Sabbath day.

There is a phrase that percolates through the self-help community: *just be 1% better every day.* This is great, except on the Sabbath. The Sabbath is a day we stop striving and remind our soul through our physical existence that we are saved by grace, not by works. For me, this means church work, chores, writing, organizing, working out, social media, educational reading, checking the news, and running errands are absent on the Sabbath. I do these things to better my existence, so on one day each week, I say, "No" to these activities.

But the Sabbath is not just a day to say no to things; it's also a day to say *yes* to the joys of life. Sabbath might mean taking long leisurely walks with the family or taking a nap in a hammock. It could mean inviting a friend over to laugh with and talk to. It can be playing or watching a game for the sake of enjoyment. It might mean praying together as a family or spending more time in scripture. Regardless of what we do or don't do, we should make sure that the Sabbath day is filled with a surplus of "Thank you, Lord!" because He has done the greatest work of all.

PREPARE TO DIE

Now, let's explore the actual work we are doing in the name of Jesus. If we feel weary doing what we believe to be the Lord's work, there's a chance we might not be accomplishing as much for God as we think. Isaiah 40 speaks that God does not grow weary and that those who hope in him won't either. In fact, they will soar on wings like eagles (Isaiah 40:28-31). So, if God doesn't grow weary and those who hope in Him won't either, a weariness of heart should give us pause.

Sure, Jesus promised that we would have trouble and persecution in this life, but weariness, burnout, and apathy don't fall into the categories of trouble and persecution. Instead, these feelings are simply indicators that our hope is not in Christ. By acknowledging them, we can move forward in adjusting our hope from the church or business we work for to the God who works over all.

If you have been involved in any religious organization, you'll already be familiar with this pattern. If not, here is a general pattern many follow. At the start of our involvement in a purpose-filled organization, there is usually great life, abundant fruit, and unquestionable revival. But over time, the passion decreases and the workload increases. Tensions often grow between individuals and groups of people within these organizations, and before we know it, what once was full of life is dead to the bone. This isn't a new problem in our world, and nobody intends for it to happen. A cursory glance on Christian schisms in history will reveal that what was once life-giving eventually loses its luster. It's a natural life cycle, just like our own physical lives. And while it sounds problematic, it's not. It's *purposeful.* This cycle is precisely God's design for His world.

We see His reasoning in Genesis 3:22: "And the Lord God said, 'The man has now become like one of us, knowing good and evil. He must not be allowed to reach out his hand and take also from the tree of life and eat, and live forever'" (NIV). The very reason that everything comes to eventual death is for our own protection. If we, or our projects, never died, we would become like God. Death makes us more dependent on God. When we feel like something that was once life-giving is now dying, we mustn't always try to keep it revived. It might be God's plan to let it die. Only then can He bring fresh life.

Jesus himself declares, "I am making everything new!" (Revelation 21:5, NIV). What is his method for making all things new? He declares His game plan in John 12:24, "Very truly I tell you, unless a kernel of wheat falls to the ground and dies, it remains only a single seed. But if it dies, it produces many seeds" (NIV). This passage seems to foreshadow Jesus' impending death. But at the same time, it offers a profound Kingdom pattern that we must follow thereafter. The principle is simple: *There is no life without death.*

If we find something life-giving, we will find something dead nearby. Ask any farmer and they'll confirm this truth; the soil full of decomposing plant and food waste will sprout the most beautiful, abundantly ripe fruits for seasons to come.

When I think of death and renewal, I think of the long history of Holy Spirit revivals at Asbury University. What has sparked these undeniable revivals time and time again? Personal confession. The revivals didn't begin with great preaching or the right music. It began the moment that people stood up and confessed their sins to others, allowing their pride to die. This confession, this dying to self, contributed to the life given by the Spirit.[12] In the Kingdom of God, death leads to life. Revival begins when something else ends.

If the work we are doing or the organization we are leading for the Kingdom has become stagnant, the question we should be asking isn't, "What more should we do?", but rather, "What needs to die?" If a person, a place, an organization, or an event cannot cease, then that could be the difference between Kingdom life and a life of monotony. To put it simply, *whatever we can't live without is our God.*

When I was studying church planting in seminary, my professor asked a question. "If you planted a church knowing that it couldn't last more than 20 years, how would that change your priorities?" My answer came immediately: My church would stay more focused on the pure mission of the Church, rather than simply building another 501c3. That simple question put everything into a laser-sharp focus for me, because a proper perspective of death is one of the greatest tools to keeping our priorities in order.

At the time of this writing, my grandparents are alive, but I've been visiting their grave for as long as I can remember. Before I was even born, they purchased their gravestone and a burial plot in the local cemetery. By the time I could walk, my grandma would take me and her other grandchildren to the cemetery (it was a small town; our destinations were limited). All growing up, my grandparents would walk their grandchildren past a gravestone that bore their names on it. The only missing element was the date of death.

Now that I am older, I can appreciate the power of such a symbol. We all know hindsight is 20/20. But what about foresight? Thinking about death won't make us die earlier, but it may make us live longer. Looking at the plot of ground in which we will be buried offers as clear a direction for our life as any. Go ahead. Take a walk in the cemetery and you'll see precisely what I mean. Nothing offers a better perspective than death.

When we start new initiatives, projects, habits, or careers we rarely ask ourselves how it will end. But I implore you, thinking about the end in the beginning leads to a life of blessing. If we are leading a business, an organization, a team, or a family, we will continually start and end things. It can become awkward if we know something needs to die in our organization, but no one is willing to admit it.

To avoid this difficulty, I often suggest that whenever we propose a new initiative or habit, we should propose a day of death in writing before we even start. This brings a healthy perspective as we grow. I know everyone wants to start something that lives forever, but we mustn't be so prideful. We cannot avoid death; we must stop trying. We should embrace that death is what brings life and seek to make our lives as full of endings as possible.

But what if we put to death something before God was finished with it? Again, this is why listening to the Holy Spirit is so important. We shouldn't throw out end dates just for the sake of it. When we prayerfully start new things, we should pray in equal measure over the death of it. If I start a new personal habit, I might set an end date for 40 days later. If I was planting a church, I would certainly set a death date for later than 40 days. All must be prayerfully considered depending on the size of the project, the habit, or the calling. But I will say this: God is more likely to end something prematurely than He is to make it last forever.

Let's say I planted a church with a death date of 15 years in the future. Within the next 15 years, the congregation experienced continual growth, baptizing more individuals every year. To some, it might feel like the church is ending at the peak of its existence and that it would be better served to remain for many years to come. But it is still in the best interest of the church to close. Why? Because in the Kingdom of God, death always brings life. Rather than enter into a life of polity, that church can now bless the start of other churches or enhance the function of other existing churches in its liquidation.

In my years of following God, I have yet to uncover a principle in scripture that blesses a person for circumventing death. Rather, there is an abundance of scripture that speaks to the blessings that come through the opposite. The Apostle Paul says in Galatians 2:20, "I have been crucified with Christ and I no longer live, but Christ lives in me. The life I now live in the body, I live by faith in the Son of God, who loved me and gave himself for me" (NIV). Let's not overlook the fact that for Christ to live in us, we have to first be crucified with Him. Whenever something dies - either spiritual or physical - there will be greater life to follow. May we cease our attempts to leave a legacy that lasts forever and start being faithful for the sake of today. We will likely not have a building with our name on it in this life, but there will be a place for us in heaven. Let's build our legacy there.

In Stephen Covey's oft-referenced book, *The 7 Habits of Highly Effective People,* he advises to "Begin with the end in mind." Covey notes, "To begin with the end in mind means to start with a clear understanding of your destination. It means to know where you're going so that you better understand where you are now and so that the steps you take are always in the right direction."[13]

When I was learning how to drive, my dad taught me the importance of knowing the direction of your destination. Quite literally: North, South, East, or West. I had to know where I was and which direction my destination was. He would say, "As long as you know the general direction of your destination, you will not get lost. You may take a few wrong turns, but you will never be far from where you were planning to go."

The end of our life matters. It is our destination. God often gives us a vision, a desire, or a passion for how our life should be at the end. However, He will rarely give us ultimate clarity on the journey. He wants us to trust Him. Let's have our idea of where we are heading, but then trust God as He leads us on the specific path. Along the way, we must faithfully start and end many, many things: relationships, habits, jobs, hobbies, and initiatives. Hold these things with open hands because life and death are in the same vicinity.

THE REJUVENATION PROJECT

Start your days at sundown. Spend 10 minutes before bed asking God what he wants to do for that day. After you feel a sense of direction, go to bed! Pray a prayer like this, "God thank you for giving me work. When I wake up, I plan to work hard for you, but in the meantime, while I rest, would you go before me working on my behalf?" Repeat this for two weeks and note any changes in your restfulness, as well as your work productivity. Prepare to be surprised.

Make GETMO a regular practice of life. We want to be excellent, but we do not want to feel the weight of "More!" Spotlight three things that you do regularly each week for your job or personal life. Can you apply the GETMO principle to any of these three things? If not, where can you apply it? I know I have emphasized the *move on* portion of the principle, but if you struggle with procrastination, you may need to take steps to progress toward "Good Enough" before you can focus your efforts on "Move on." Before you decide where to place your efforts first, ask your spouse or a close friend which one they feel you should prioritize. They will likely identify your weakness in .5 seconds.

Establish a Sabbath day. Mark out a 24-hour period that is to be holy. (For me, that is Friday at 7pm to Saturday at 7pm.) Throughout your Sabbath, do no ordinary work. Establishing a new rhythm is not going to happen in a week; it is a learned skill. If you can't completely overhaul your day, just begin little by little. Once you have marked out the time frame, start by determining one thing to say no to, such as chores, email, or social media. Then, say yes to something like taking a nap. Repeat for a few weeks until you can add another thing to say no to or yes to. Over the course of six months of gradually adding to and subtracting from the Sabbath day, you will notice that your day is set aside as holy, and that the grace of God that blesses that day will run over into all your life.

What needs to die? Write out some of the activities you are doing in your personal life, or if you are leading an organization, write out what, specifically, you are doing in your organization. Ask the Holy Spirit if anything needs to die. Don't rely on your own instincts. Really listen to God here, because you only want things to die that He wants to die. That's what will bring new life. In my own personal life, whenever I'm faced with a new opportunity, I look at what might need to die. I don't have unlimited abilities. I am human. If I take a volunteer opportunity, it means that I may need to quit another one. If I'm picking up a part time job, my wife might need to end her part time job. Attempt to live by the principle that if you bring something new in, you'll likely need to send something out.

CHAPTER TWELVE

THE GARDENER PRUNES AND GRAFTS

CREATION REGULARLY GIVES testimony to the ways of God in heaven. Consider the water cycle: It isn't just a natural phenomena, but it also represents how the Word of God moves through our world (Isaiah 55:10-11). Therefore, it is of no surprise that The Rejuvenated Life is exemplified throughout creation. On the last night of Jesus' life, He uses nature to give one of the most visually profound pictures of our connection with God. Jesus says:

> "I am the true vine, and my Father is the gardener. He cuts off every branch in me that bears no fruit, while every branch that does bear fruit he prunes so that it will be even more fruitful. You are already clean because of the word I have spoken to you. Remain in me, as I also remain in you. No branch can bear fruit by itself; it must remain in the vine. Neither can you bear fruit unless you remain in me. I am the vine; you are the branches. If you remain in me and I in you, you will bear much

> fruit; apart from me you can do nothing. If you do not remain in me, you are like a branch that is thrown away and withers; such branches are picked up, thrown into the fire and burned. (John 15:1-6, NIV)

Jesus's teaching here is simple, so I dare not over complicate the analogy. Jesus is the vine. We are the branches. The Father is the Gardener. To put this analogy into perspective, it's important to note that, while we are the *visual* part of the plant, we provide no real nutrients or structural support. A branch with its leaves exists to receive light from the sun, and to turn that light into useful energy for the plant. Spiritually speaking, if Jesus is the light (John 8:12) and the vine (John 5:15), He's got photosynthesis on lockdown. We are, simply put, the part of the plant that brings beauty, fullness, and depth, but we are not the main structure of the plant. Jesus is our roots and our structure. He is the light we need. He is our source of nutrients. In short, we are nothing without Him. His instruction to us is to simply remain with Him. Without remaining, we are like a branch without roots: *debris*.

Last summer, we Midwesterners experienced a storm that brought near-100 mph winds and caused incredible damage. I, like homeowners and neighbors all across the city, cleaned up my yard of piles and piles of storm debris. But a few weeks later, I noticed there was still more to be done: broken limbs were hanging in my trees. The limbs, at first, had blended in, but soon I could see the leaves changing color; large swaths of brown leaves against the backdrop of green. Although the branches were occupying the same space, some were full of life and some were dead. The limbs that weren't connected to the tree were unable to sustain life. All throughout that summer, if a stiff breeze blew in the late afternoon, large, dead limbs fell into my yard. Even today, some damaged branches are still hanging in my tree - and may be for many years - dead, lifeless, and unattached to their source of life.

It doesn't matter how close to Jesus we *appear* to be; only through a roots-deep connection will we be sustained and bear fruit. Maybe we assume we weathered a tough season because we're still in proximity to Jesus through church or volunteerism or giving. The truth is, many followers of Christ - and yes, even pastors - become disconnected from Jesus far before they fall away from Him. It takes time to recognize that disconnection because everything appears normal on the outside. But over time - just like the fading, dying branches in my storm-damaged trees - we wither.

The good news: unlike my storm-damaged branches, there is hope. Our God is a master gardener, and reconnection to the source is ever-possible through repentance. Repentance, simply put, is willingness to change. Any one of us who is unwilling to repent and change their heart will be cut off from our life source by the Father. A life without repentance is a life without Jesus.

In the Bible, King David is well known for being a man dearly loved by God and who dearly loved God. Even though he often wrestled with some deep personal issues, King David is crowned with a title many of us seek: *a man after God's own heart*. Why such honor and praise, even after a running list of some pretty serious offenses? King David, although far from sinless, was practiced in one thing: repenting quickly, and often.

In 2 Samuel 12, David is confronted by the prophet Nathan for his terrible sins of adultery and murder. David's immediate response? "I have sinned against the Lord" (2 Samuel 12:13, NIV). Let's contrast this to his predecessor King Saul. God instructs Saul to destroy a wicked group of people *completely*, leaving nothing alive. Saul does most of what God asks of him, but leaves some of the prized sheep and captures their king alive. The prophet Samuel confronts Saul for his sin in not obeying the word of God completely. His response? "But I did obey the Lord" (1 Samuel 15:20, NIV). Both Kings did wrong, but one made an excuse and one repented quickly. The man of God is the one who repents, not the one who seeks to clarify their actions.

This level of character does not happen by accident. We do not have a biological bent to act like Christ. But, while we, as branches, are structurally different from our roots in Christ, we are still the same organism. We are one. Just as oak leaves do not grow on pine trees, branches reflect what they are connected to. Thus, to remain with Jesus Christ is to look like Jesus Christ. To get there, we must approach our sins with a repentant heart. This takes the determination of a soul as we actively participate in change, repent routinely, and remain in Christ.

Many of us associate repentance with guilt and shame, conjuring up the childhood embarrassment we sometimes felt when repenting of our sins at an early age. But repentance is about far more than sin and confession. Repentance is the vehicle we use *to become like Christ.*

At first, repentance almost exclusively involves the confessing of and turning away from the standard sins outlined in scripture. This is good, and when paired with daily cleansing through the Word, is essential for breaking free from sin's strongholds. But this is not where repenting ends. We are on a continuous quest to become like Christ. This journey doesn't just involve the removal of every obvious sin we discuss in churches, but sometimes, involves things specific to our own life.

This is why, the more we die to ourselves and become like Christ, we might find ourselves repenting of seemingly good things, like idolizing "family time" because we are worshiping our family more than our God. Repentance is not about getting rid of sin; it is about *changing everything in our lives to be just like Jesus.* The longer we follow Christ with a heart posture of repentance, the more He will invite us to give up and change things in our lives that we once thought were normal, or right, or even good. If we are unwilling to repent or change at any point in our walk with Christ, we will become cut off from the source of life. We will wither. We will burn out. Like a branch swaying to the whisper of God's gentle breeze, we must remain. We must follow. Our job is to simply obey and change whenever God brings something to our attention.

I grew up loving sports, especially baseball. Specifically, the two sports teams I loved most were the Chicago Cubs and the Notre Dame Fighting Irish. They were also my dad's favorite teams, so we had a lot of great bonding moments over these teams. For twenty years, I was a fanatic. And then, I wasn't. In 2021, I felt the

Spirit of God requesting more of my devotion towards Him. Allocating more devotion to any area of our life will require us to sacrifice in another, and in this instance, God knew where to draw it from: Notre Dame and the Cubs. How was I to do this? I felt God kindly instruct me to remove all clothing and signage from my house that represented a sports team I never played for. In obedience, I did it. (He did allow me to keep one Cubs hat because my wife bought it for me and in my heart, I associate that hat with her and not the Cubs.)

Of course, we could all argue that there is nothing wrong with enjoying the Cubs and Notre Dame. To my knowledge, supporting these teams is not sinful, and, in fact, I have some of the fondest memories based around them. But Jesus is drawing me ever closer towards Himself. And, at first, that might look like repenting of lust or pride or sloth, but before we know it, that might look like repenting of your Fighting Irish idols. Wherever we are on our repentance road, remember this: We are not the one in charge of making ourselves look like Jesus. That is the Gardener's job. So, I wouldn't encourage us to make up what we need to repent of. Instead, we must be open to pruning by the Gardener, and do what we are led to do when we are led to do it.

The branches do not tell the Gardener how to do His job. The Gardener is the one that prunes, cutting away parts to make the whole organism healthy. If we don't listen to the voice of God, we may prune something that God meant for life or we may accept something as wholesome that is actually killing us. (More on that in a second.) Repentance will be specific to each of our lives, but only God knows which habits, interests, or activities we need to change.

We mustn't become Pharisees, making our own human policies and rules for repentance. Only God can tell us what we need to repent of. In our early walk with God, scripture offers a clear guide for what God is asking of us. After all, the 10 commandments are still perfect standards of God's nature today. But as we continue to grow in our faith, the Holy Spirit offers us deeper direction, guidance, and instruction to apply those scriptures to our life. God doesn't say in scripture, "Don't have a Cubs license plate on your car." He does say, "You shall not make for yourself an idol in the form of anything in the heavens above, on the earth below, or in the waters beneath" (Exodus 20:4, NIV). In my case, the Holy Spirit helped show me what was stealing my devotion to God, and I knew it was true because of what God has clearly laid out in scripture.

As we move up the mountain of God, we need to be more tuned into His voice rather than the voices of those around us. God may ask us to give up something that He is not asking anyone else to give up. We mustn't look around at others and get bitter or make excuses. Just repent and obey. The repentance God wants from us goes far beyond right and wrong. We must open our minds to surrender *anything* that causes us to be different or disconnected from Jesus. This process doesn't start and end at the moment of our salvation; God is gracious enough to lead us over time. But here's what I know to be true: We will never graduate from repenting. If you haven't changed anything at God's request in a while, you may be as dead as the storm-torn branches propped up in my tree. Don't delay: repent and remain.

GRAFTING

Our Gardener is not just interested in eliminating decay from our lives; He also desires to add good nutrients to it. In this way, our God grafts us. Grafting is the process of taking two separate organisms and merging them into one. We see this with plants of all kinds, or even our skin in times of surgery. While many of us are aware of the pruning God offers for our lives, we rarely pause to consider His generous grafting. Paul talks of grafting in Romans 11:18-21:

> But you must not brag about being grafted in to replace the branches that were broken off. You are just a branch, not the root. "Well," you may say, "those branches were broken off to make room for me." Yes, but remember—

> those branches were broken off because they didn't believe in Christ, and you are there because you do believe. So don't think highly of yourself, but fear what could happen. For if God did not spare the original branches, he won't spare you either. (NLT)

To offer context, this scripture is specifically discussing the relationship between the Jews and the Gentiles. Gentiles felt they were of great importance because God had ingrafted them into the tree of life alongside the Jews. Paul's caution, however, is not to become impressed by our own branches, but by what we are connected to. God is able to graft *any* person into the family tree of God as if they had been there all along. That is the beauty of God's design. And while this particular scripture speaks of grafting as a clear picture of salvation, the process is also a deeply moving spiritual principle.

You may have heard the advice that you're the average of the five people you hang around the most and the books you read. There is truth in this wisdom, but few of us know why. The reason is *grafting*. In the same way that God grafts us into His family tree by the blood of Jesus, we are routinely being grafted with the character and skills of those around us. God uses this process to give us good things from Him. Similar to the exchange of money, when God blesses us with a gift, it will likely come through the hands of another person. In this way, more people are touched by God in the process. A more common word we use for this process is *impartation*.

Impartation is commonly understood as the laying of hands to pass a spiritual gift on to someone else. 1 Timothy 4:14 says, "Do not neglect your gift, which was given you through prophecy when the body of elders laid their hands on you" (NIV). An undeniable supernatural reality is that spiritual gifts, talents, skills, temperaments, attitudes, and even faith itself can be passed from person to person like a physical commodity.

Certainly in your life someone has come up to you and said, "You act just like your dad." or "That's exactly what your mother would have done in that situation." Our behaviors are not simply predisposed in our DNA. Rather, our behaviors are learned from the people we are in greatest proximity to and authority under.

The principle is this: God gave us purposeful gifts from day one of conception, but He also routinely brings people into our lives to give more gifts and build the full picture of our destiny. We will not mature into our full purpose in a vacuum. The people in our life are not an accident. God brings people towards each other to edify each other. Community is not just a trendy word on a church sign; it is the lifeblood of our destiny.

There are three ways that impartation takes place in our lives where God gives intangible things from one person to another: (1) laying of hands, (2) sitting under someone's teaching, and (3) proximity.

Truthfully, the laying of hands is the most difficult for me to explain, but I see it too many times to discredit. Specifically, this impartation has transformed my life. Once, when I was struggling to hear the voice of God in my life, my mentor laid his hands on me. He prayed that God might give me whatever he had in his life so that I may hear the voice of God. Guess what? I heard *instantly*. The laying of hands felt like a head start in my faith journey.

When I got married, unashamedly, one of my favorite moments was opening all of our wedding cards full of well-wishes and money and gift cards. Like most newlyweds, my wife and I were starting our life together without a lot to our name. The money people passed along to us gave us a good start in life. There are so many things we didn't know we needed when we started living on our own, and that money bridged the gap toward a healthy financial beginning. While we, of course, no longer live off wedding gifts, those gifts provided a head start while our income caught up for us to build a life together.

When it comes to the laying of hands, the same is true: we won't live off it forever, but it's a beautiful head start. While we can't live our spiritual lives on the back of someone else's righteousness, we mustn't neglect or underestimate the laying of hands. When I am prayed for, the Spirit of God that rests on the other person rests on me for a short season. The impartation through the laying of hands may "wear off" eventually, but the goal is that by the time it does, we are now standing with the same Spirit stewarded in us.

I have heard, seen, and experienced people laying hands on someone and giving a passion for the Word of God. Immediately, someone who was apathetic to scripture is invigorated with - and for - God's Word. This anointing may last only a short time, unless the person establishes their own passion for God's Word. In that case, they will never be the same. If we use the laying of hands as a jump start rather than a crutch, we will abound in many good things.

Impartation also happens through submission to someone's teaching. I have a mentor in my life that I have never met in person. Through the power of digital media, I have sat under the regular teaching of another pastor. I didn't seek this person because of popularity, but when I was introduced to the sermons and listened for the first time, I came alive in my spirit and God spoke to me: *I have made you in a similar way to this man. Listen to him and gather it in.* The pastor I listen to doesn't know I exist, yet he has imparted a great many things to my life. Clearly, there is no physical laying of hands, but as my heart listens to wisdom with submissiveness and openness, I am able to receive the wisdom - and it *sticks*. Some of his teachings are understood and applied immediately, and others are hidden away in my heart for a later season. While it certainly matters who is teaching us, it also matters that we are open to what is being taught. Like the Parable of the Sower that Jesus described in Mark 4, we must hear and accept the teaching to receive it.

Who we listen to matters as much as *what* we listen to. Is this person or outlet teaching hope? Fear? Distrust? Disobedience? Holiness? Learning is counterproductive if we are hearing and accepting the fear-based discussion that goes on regularly in our media consumption. (Of note: I have yet to meet a person that is full of faith but also consumes 24-hour news.)

When my daughter was one month old, she became very sick with a virus and was struggling to breath. She was admitted to the

Pediatric ICU immediately, as she struggled for the most basic necessity of life: oxygen. The doctor talked to us about the process of her treatment and uttered these words: "It will likely get worse before it gets better." I was shocked. "She can barely breathe," I thought. "What could be worse than that?"

I sat down to send a text updating my family of her condition. At the end of my text, I wrote, "The doctor said it will likely get worse before it gets better." But my spirit felt convicted at that last phrase. I knew what the doctor said, but was I going to agree with him? I immediately deleted my last sentence and instead, I simply wrote, "Pray that she breathes."

Looking back now, she never got worse before she got better. *She simply just got better.* Did I have a misinformed doctor? Not at all. The nurses informed me he was one of the best they ever saw, and he did great things for my daughter. But while my wife and I *heard* what the doctor said, we didn't *accept* it. We, instead, accepted the testimony of a dear friend that regularly spoke over his young daughter with cancer, saying "You will have life not death." I saw the healing of his daughter and believed it would be the same for my own. And now, both our daughters are living and healthy.

Certainly, there are more complexities to life than just believing what we want to believe and assuming it will be true, but we would all be surprised by how often what we accept from others correlates to our life. May I offer a gentle reminder? *We do not have to submit to everything that is presented to us as fact.* We are always being presented with good news and bad news, wisdom and folly. Choose wisely what you accept, because both can be grafted to your life.

The final discernable way of impartation is through proximity, which is more commonly called discipleship. Likely, the most influential people in our life impacted us not because they sat us down for a teaching, but because we had the opportunity to observe them in daily life. Maybe discipleship is more osmosis than interjection - a seeping of one soul to another through proximity. This is the brand of impartation Jesus seemed to live out with his 12 disciples. Some things are best caught, not taught. This is why community matters. Our physical community *and* our digital community. It is all grafting onto us. If God has placed someone into our life to impart wisdom to us, our spirit will leap like John the Baptist in the womb. May we receive everything that God wants to give us through them.

PRUNING THE GRAFTING

Here is where this all connects in our life. We understand that God wants to prune our lives to look like Jesus. We also recognize that we are in continual grafting of either God's will or the world. And so, the combination we desperately want to avoid is grafting things into our lives that God just has to turn around and prune. This cycle makes many of us feel like we are spinning our wheels because God has to routinely counter the poor choices we make in our lives.

I once had a young man in my youth group announce to me that he had decided to pick up cursing. This is definitely an interesting behavioral choice for a young man to logically decide to partake in, so I asked him about it. He said, "Well, I started working construction and all my coworkers do it, so now it just comes naturally." I told him that, while I truly didn't care if he'd decided to mix in some four-letter words into his language, he should count the cost. I asked him, "When you have a 16-year-old someday, are you going to let him cuss in your house?" He said, "Absolutely not!" I said, "Then I suggest you think again about starting something that you are just going to have to quit later on."

Friends, let's stop adding things to our lives that God just has to turn around and take away. This happens in many, many ways. People come to church desiring freedom from anxiety, depression, low self-esteem, lust, fear, anger, and the like, and yet, we continually feed our lives these very things. Let me be very clear: God wants us free just as much as we want to be. But at some point we have to stop grafting on the very things God is trying to free us from. Want to have a positive outlook on life? Prune your gossipy friends and sit in solitude outside. Want to have a higher self-esteem? Prune social media and start moving your body. Want to live without fear? Stop listening to the news or people talking about the news and memorize scripture instead. Want freedom from depression? Turn off Netflix and open the Word of God. Tired of being addicted to pornography? Take a baseball bat to your phone and get a flip phone. What if, instead of grafting things into our lives that God has to prune later, we actually let God do the pruning *and* grafting?

Instead of just asking what God wants to take away from us, what if we prayed, "God what do you want to *add* to my life?" We would be surprised by how many more out-of-the-blue encounters with great people we would have. It would blow our minds to discover how many incredible books would fall into our laps. Opportunities would abound! If the process of pruning is repenting, then the process of grafting is surrender. We must surrender our choices and free will. If Jesus is Lord, let's submit fully to Him. Let's no longer do what feels right to us, but what the Spirit leads us to do. If we can align with what God is pruning and grafting, we will see God move in our lives like never before.

God is a good gardener. May we repent and surrender our hearts to allow Him to prune and to graft. If we can submit to God and the people He gives us, we can more confidently walk in God's best for our life as we grow forward in faith.

THE REJUVENATION PROJECT

What needs to be pruned? Don't ask yourself, ask the Father. In my experience, He usually answers this prayer quickly - and it will likely be uncomfortable. Don't assume that what God will ask you to eliminate will be a bad thing. He may ask you to give up a good thing because your attachment to it is unhealthy. I once had God ask me to repent of how much I prided myself on spending time with Him. He told me to give up my quiet time with Him for a short period to realize how I had become prideful in my own efforts for spiritual discipline. I am telling you: *there is nothing off limits for repentance*. Get on your knees, repent, and change your thinking. The way to remain in Christ is repentance.

What is currently being imparted on your life? Who are the people you are in closest proximity to? What teaching are you sitting under? Who has something in their life that you admire? Evaluate each of these areas of grafting. Seek out the people you admire. Be wary of those that consume and believe mistruths. Open up your heart and mind when wisdom flows from a teacher. Surrender all you have to God. Open hands is the posture of pruning and grafting.

CHAPTER THIRTEEN

SHUT UP AND PRAY

PRAYER IS MOST often described as talking to God. I do not disagree, but certainly the power of prayer lies far beyond simple speech (James 5:16). In fact, prayer might be more wholly defined as *communication* with God. Communication involves more modes than just words. Body language, tone, speed, or inflection are all important methods we rely on to help convey the meaning behind our words. Communication also involves the two-way exchange of information from person to person. Just because one person is talking doesn't mean the other is listening. Great communication places a higher emphasis on the receiving of information than on the giving of information. These distinctions are important to note as we discuss prayer, because powerful prayers come through a fuller understanding of communication with God.

Why do we communicate with God? To get on the same page. What makes prayer powerful is not the talking; it's the *getting on the same page*. Sure, we can have dreams for our life and ask God to fulfill them. And God can have dreams for our life and can choose to fulfill those instead. But the real dynamite combination is when the dreams and desires that we want for our life are the same dreams and desires that God wants for our life. *That's* when prayer takes off.

For some, prayer is relied on only in situations of great peril. For others, it is a more common practice. Regardless of our rations and reasons for prayer, we must recognize this truth: *prayer is not our time to persuade God*. In fact, prayer is persuading ourselves to be more like God. Like a married couple that barely needs words to communicate, we, too, should desire a shared wavelength with our creator. The closer we are to someone, the more we can communicate beyond words. We should desire to be so close with our creator that few words are necessary. We should become so intertwined with God that we don't know where we begin and where He ends, or where we end and He begins.

As we align our hearts with God's through prayer, it's worth noting that ambiguity abounds. While there will be moments that God sovereignly acts in our lives with or without our prayers, there will also be moments where our requests are instrumental in moving the hand of God. There isn't a secret formula for revealing the precise ways our participation in prayer will affect our circumstances. In my life, I can see times when my specific prayer mattered immensely, and other times where God worked despite even a breath of petition. So, what's the secret sauce? What works best? And how? While no human is privy to the omniscience of God, I do know this: a simple "thank you" goes a long way.

The Apostle Paul says, "Rejoice always, pray continually, give thanks in all circumstances; for this is God's will for you in Christ Jesus" (1 Thessalonians 5:16-18, NIV). Oh the perplexing "pray continually" passage. Is it possible? Is it not? Must we become a monk to make it happen? The interesting thing about this passage is that the scripture indicates three different acts, but uses the word *this*, not *these*, to quantify them. Grammar rules suggest the passage should read, "*These* are God's will for you," since there are three distinct actions listed, but instead, Paul seems to lump them all into one combo. Perhaps the reason is this: rejoicing, continual prayer, and thankfulness are closely related, if not inseparable. The combination can't be turned on and off, or dialed back, or switched back and forth between the three. Rejoicing, prayer, and gratitude should not be thought of as something we do, but rather something we *are*.

How? Through unconscious prayer. There are at least two kinds of prayers: conscious prayer and unconscious prayer. We are more familiar with conscious prayer, but it is our unconscious prayer that really moves the needle in heaven. We pray the conscious prayers, and the Spirit prays the unconscious prayers on our behalf.

> In the same way, the Spirit helps us in our weakness. We do not know what we ought to pray for, but the Spirit himself intercedes for us through wordless groans. And he who searches our hearts knows the mind of the Spirit, because the Spirit intercedes for God's people in accordance with the will of God. (Romans 8:26-27, NIV)

Who do you think prays more effectively: us or the Holy Spirit? I'm going to bet on the Holy Spirit all day long. If we're depending on Him for so much already, we might as well hand him our lackluster prayer life, too.

The truth is, most prayer lives can be defined as just that: lackluster. At no point in my life has my prayer life ever felt strong, yet scripture says that God helps us in our weakness by picking up where we cannot even comprehend. God is not surprised by our inability to pray from a place of strength, which is why He steps in. While prayer has so often been referred to as a conversation with God (and it can be, yes), the Holy Spirit's intercession seems to defy such a simple definition. There is far more to prayer than merely talking back and forth. In fact, I dare say the prayers that move mountains in our lives are the ones we don't even realize we are praying, the ones in which the Spirit prays on our behalf.

So, what's the key to praying these miraculous prayers? Well, our command is to rejoice, pray, and give thanks. For us to steward the continual prayers of the Spirit on our behalf, we must also steward a heart of praise and thanksgiving. The more we fill our mouths and minds with praise and gratitude, the stronger our prayer life will be. Likewise, the more we speak unwholesome talk, the more difficult it will be for the Spirit to pray on our behalf.

If we don't yet see the supernatural workings of God in our personal life, it may be because we have shut down the Spirit from praying for us continually. Ask yourself: Am I grieving the Holy Spirit who is praying on my behalf?

> Do not let any unwholesome talk come out of your mouths, but only what is helpful for building others up according to their needs, that it may benefit those who listen. *And do not grieve the Holy Spirit of God*, with whom you were sealed for the day of redemption. Get rid of all bitterness, rage and anger, brawling and slander, along with every form of malice. Be kind and compassionate to one another, forgiving each other, just as in Christ God forgave you. (Ephesians 4:29-32, NIV)

In the middle of this passage, there is a command to not grieve the Holy Spirit, sandwiched between commands that rely heavily on keeping a tight rein on our tongue. This arrangement suggests that our words play a pretty important role in not grieving the Holy Spirit. We are familiar with our words playing an important part in our prayer life, but what if the words we *didn't* say were more important than the words we *did* say? Eliminating gossip, slander, coarse joking, anger, and the like from our mouths can do more to free up the Holy Spirit's work in our life, allowing us to pray from a place of strength due to the Holy Spirit, rather than a place of weakness because of our humanity.

When we are weak, He is strong. We must rely on the Holy Spirit to do our heavy lifting in prayer. By recognizing that what we do *not* say is more important than what we do say, we are setting the foundation for every prayer endeavor to come. Often, we are encouraged to utilize prayer to ask God for things in our lives. But truthfully, I desire for my heart to be so surrendered to God and His plans that I dare not wish for anything else but Him. I don't want God to follow *my* plans, I want to follow *God's* plans.

God knows what we want more than we do. When we surrender our prayer lives to the Holy Spirit and loosen the grip on our list of prayer requests, we will find a life designed beyond our wildest imagination. If we're honest, there are things happening in our lives today that are setting us up for a future we don't even know how to ask for. We cannot depend on ourselves to see the bigger picture, and often God won't reveal it on our own timeline. While we can certainly continue to pray for what we don't understand, we would do better to delegate the mystery to the Holy Spirit to work on our behalf in His infinite strength.

Does this delegation mean we should never carve out time to pray? Quite the contrary. Prayer is an essential part of a rejuvenated and fruitful life and should be practiced regularly. All I have suggested is that we needn't talk so much. Instead of talking in our time of prayer, let's try shutting up.

I have felt a lot of guilt in the past for not having the words to say when I prayed alone with God. My mind would often be too distracted to finish a conscious thought. I would overanalyze my prayer, wondering if the few words I did say were the right ones. Often, I would end up just sitting. At the time, I thought I was messing up, but I now know I may have had a better handle on prayer than I realized.

Many of the deepest times of prayer I have experienced involved me just sitting. Shutting up. Silence. Despite my few words for Him, the evidence of God in my life has grown stronger over time. I now accept more confidently the truth Jesus says in Matthew 6:7-8, "And when you pray, do not keep on babbling like pagans, for they think they will be heard because of their many words. Do not be like them, for your Father knows what you need before you ask him" (NIV).

Prayer can feel so misleading. We feel like prayer is all on us and all about our words, and in reality, our strongest prayers are all on Him and without any words at all. No wonder we don't see the power of prayer! We haven't yet tapped into the true power. Even our prayers are fully dependent on God. We must only ensure nothing unwholesome comes out of our mouth that would prohibit the prayers of the Spirit in our lives. If we turn off the unwholesome talk and turn up the gratitude and rejoicing, we will increase a flow of blessing that only the Holy Spirit could pray over our life.

ASKING AND DREAMING

When I was in college, my faith grew to new levels as I was really grasping the scriptures more in my heart. I had the realization that I needed to see miracles in my life like Jesus and the disciples did. So, I began to pray for God to perform miracles through me. I prayed religiously for a power that was anything but religious. I did see miracles begin to happen, but my life wasn't any more peaceful or trusting in God. In fact, I would argue the times I saw miracles first happen, I became as prideful as ever. I cared and prayed more for the works of God than to know God Himself. I wish I would have realized my error earlier.

Ironically, when I started writing this chapter, I wanted to write about dreaming big for the Kingdom of God. But, in truth, if our requests and dreams are about anything other than growing more surrendered and in love with God, we have missed the greatest dream imaginable. When Jesus did pray for himself in John 17, He prays to be glorified. Without knowing the context, this would seem like a pretty selfish prayer. But when we understand that He prays this prayer the night before He is killed for the sins of the world, the tone changes. This glory that Jesus prayed for could only be attained by the greatest level of surrender and submission this world has ever seen. Likewise, our wildest dream or aspiration that we wish to pray for is best accomplished by the absolute laying down of our life to God's will and plan.

If we desire to do great things for God, I believe God put that in us. The way to see those dreams come true is not by praying for God to make those dreams come true, but rather to pray for the emphatic surrender of our life to Him. Realize this: If God put a wholesome dream in us, He probably already wants to accomplish it! But our pride can block His glory. Jesus' prayer to be glorified is wrapped in a thick layer of surrender as He understood the way to glory was through a grave. Big dreams don't call for big prayers. Big dreams call for humble pray-ers. Be a follower of Christ who dies to pride so that God can raise you up for His ultimate glory.

When we desire more of God and dream of seeking Him alone, He gives everything in response. We do not need to feel responsible for dreaming and praying for big things for our lives; we need to be so lost in His love that we never look anywhere else. You think I am discounting dreaming big? If my dream is God, it doesn't get any bigger than that.

I am reminded of Matthew 6:33, "But seek first his kingdom and his righteousness, and all these things will be given to you as well" (NIV). If God is not our dream and He is not our ask, then we need to stop whatever we're doing and learn to sit with our mouth closed until we realize that *everything comes from Him and is for Him*. Even when we have a great big idea to pray for, God gave us the idea in the first place. I am not trying to diminish our worth; I am trying to lift higher His worth!

I am a little embarrassed to admit this, but my prayer life changed as I was replacing the roof on my house. My friends and I had just finished installing a metal roof on my house, so I had many extra pieces and various lengths of metal to dispose of, along with the oversized box it was all delivered in. I didn't have a truck to transport the waste, nor anywhere to get rid of the materials myself. I was a little annoyed at how I was going to clean up this huge mess we'd made. I was working and not thinking about God at all when I uttered in my head, "I wish somebody would just randomly come with a truck and take all these scraps and the shipping crate and pay me for it." To be clear, this wasn't a prayer; it was just a thought. A few minutes later, I posted the scraps on Facebook Marketplace. The next day, a man messaged me, asking if he could come and take the scraps and leftovers *and* he helped me return the shipping crate the materials came in. Not only that, but he paid me after it was all done!

I was baffled and humbled. Not the false humility kind, either. *Truly humbled*, weak before the Lord. At that moment, I realized there wasn't a word or thought I could utter in the universe that God didn't already know. I wish I had a more holy example of God's nearness than a heap of metal scraps, but hey, I guess God can use anything.

God's response to my roofing woes were of no benefit to anyone but me (and the man's chickens that got a sweet new coop with the leftover metal) and yet, God was still willing to work in it. This was not a life or death scenario. It was simply a convenience, a secret wish of mine that felt so shallow I would have never dared prayed for it on my own will. But God had no trouble connecting - and creating - exactly what I desired to happen. If God was willing to work in something so minute, I imagine He would work in about any situation. It doesn't take a special chant to get God to answer a prayer. It takes a heart that is submitted in all things to the Spirit. In all things, at all times. We cannot have a separate prayer life from our real life. It all has to be for Him.

We will see transformation in our lives when we recognize that God hears us *always*, not just when we pray. This is why eliminating unwholesome talk matters so immensely. God sees our life as worship of and to Him. Imagine you're at church and the worship leader paused her Sunday morning set to lead us all in a collective round of gossip. That would certainly stifle the worship tone, wouldn't it? The effect is just the same in our everyday lives when we participate in unwholesome talk. Whatever praise was on our lips is now made salty by an untamed tongue.

Fresh water and salt water don't come from the same river. Likewise, we cannot have powerful prayers and unwholesome talk come from the same mouth. If we mix fresh water with salt water, we will have salt water. If we mix powerful, eloquent prayers with unwholesome talk, God will hear unwholesome talk.

Do not grieve the Holy Spirit of God who is in you. Let Him run free and loose in your life. When you pray, you needn't even know what you are asking for. Just submit a short prayer of gratitude and then rest in His presence. Do not take yourself more seriously than you ought to. Even your greatest moment of strength doesn't compare to the mighty power of the Spirit that rose Jesus from the grave. May He be our desire and dream. May He be our plan A. May He be what we depend on. May He be the center of our lives. May we steward His presence in our lives and not grieve Him. This is the power of God for all people.

WHEN WORDS MATTER

I have just suggested to you that the most powerful prayer life is the unconscious one where you allow the Holy Spirit to cover your weakness and pray on your behalf. However, there is another aspect of prayer in which God seems to rely more on the conscious prayers of people. We call this intercession, where we pray on behalf of other people. Intercession is *powerful.* When I pray conscious prayers for myself, it seems like nothing huge happens. When I pray for others? It's like heaven can't be stopped.

Don't be confused by this, nor underestimate the power of a community praying together. It falls in line with God's ways. God has a pattern of making sure no one can take credit for their own work. Our conscious prayers for ourselves might not do much, but our conscious prayers for others can move mountains. Think about it like this: The people who have the best perspective are often on the outside of a situation. God often taps on these outside people to pray because they are most likely to see the reality of the situation and pray to the true heart of God.

In all things, God loves relationships and unity. When the Holy Spirit prays for us and we see Him at work, our relationship with the Spirit is strengthened. When we pray for others and we see it work, our relationship with them is strengthened just the same. The power of prayer in a community of people encourages humility, honesty, submission, and far more. Do not expect to take care of yourself in your prayer life. Instead, submit this work to the Holy Spirit. Then, take care of others with your conscious prayers.[14]

THE REJUVENATION PROJECT.

The highest priority in this assignment is to clean up your unwholesome talk. This will be the foundation for a prayer life that is effective and glorifying to God. Don't believe you are off the hook if you don't cuss; I am not talking about just cursing. The worst offense is often the harsh words we say about others. Eliminate gossip and slander from your life and begin to speak kindly of - and to - others.

Devote a time of prayer for yourself where you pray in complete silence. This creates a dependency on the Holy Spirit. Words are most necessary in prayer for praise, thanksgiving, repentance, and intercession. If your prayers don't fall in those categories, lean not on your words, but on the Spirit. Remember: prayer is not talking, it's communicating. We can understand a lot about a situation by just sitting. Not only that, sitting in silence gives us a better ability to receive information from God. We must get good at sitting!

If sitting is a challenge for you, I suggest you set a timer for one minute and sit. The following day, set a timer for two minutes and sit. The next day three minutes, then four minutes, then five. Do this until you have become comfortable sitting for longer periods of time. Try to at least get comfortable sitting for thirty minutes in solitude. Using that simple method, you'll be at that level in a month. In the long run, we don't want to use a timer to measure our time with God, but to start, it is a helpful practice. Over time, we will be able to sense from the Holy Spirit if we need to sit longer or shorter.

Finally, pay attention to the times in which someone specific comes to your mind. Simply pray for that person with conscious words. Don't ever hesitate to lift your voice to heaven on behalf of another individual. You may never know the impact your prayer carries in the lives of those you're interceding for.

CHAPTER FOURTEEN

WE CAN'T OUTGIVE GOD

UP TO THIS point we have been surrendering, trusting, listening, washing, pruning, forgiving, grafting, and the like; and I hope you are starting to feel the blessing of The Rejuvenated Life. However, if you are still not prospering or refreshed, might I suggest a likely culprit? "A generous person will prosper; whoever refreshes others will be refreshed" (Proverbs 11:25, NIV). This is a promise of scripture. If we want to be refreshed, we must refresh others. If we want to prosper, we have to give. Thus, living a refreshed and prosperous life is completely in our control. We needn't have a PhD to our name, or a fancy job title, or a wall full of plaques. To live a refreshed and prosperous life, we need one key element: *generosity*.

Most of us tend to assume we're already fairly generous. We round up our change at the checkout line and give a few extra pennies to cancer research or community theater. We send checks to disaster relief funds. We pass along hand-me-down clothing to a Christian resale store or buy Girl Scout Cookies from the little girl knocking on our door. But does this qualify as a spirit of generosity? Not exactly.

> As Jesus looked up, he saw the rich putting their gifts into the temple treasury. He also saw a poor widow put in two very small copper coins. "Truly I tell you," he said, "this poor widow has put in more than all the others. All these people gave their gifts out of their wealth; but she

> out of her poverty put in all she had to live on." (Luke 21:1-4, NIV)

Jesus has a knack for teaching the unexpected. When it comes to numbers, math is math, right? Shouldn't the larger amount given equal the greater gift? But Jesus isn't explaining the earthly reality of arithmetic. He is teaching us about heaven. In heaven, quantities are irrelevant. There is no such thing as a quantifiable measure of pure generosity. Generosity can't be displayed in a receipt of our charitable giving at the end of each year. Generosity is a position of the heart, not the checkbook. It's a *state*, not a statement.

If the promise of scripture is that those who are generous will be prosperous and refreshed, then we must actively employ generosity as a key means to fighting against burnout. And when I say generosity, I am talking about *money*. For many years, well-intentioned people have been robbing others of a prosperous and refreshed life by making claims that we don't have to give money, but that we can give time instead. This is deception. Generosity must involve our money or possessions: things you can see, feel, need, and want. Service, on the other hand, is when we physically show up and volunteer our time for a specific outcome. Let me be clear: both are noble. Both are important. But they are not the same. When we think about generosity, we must think about money or valuable possessions.

So why is giving so important? It prioritizes our heart. The two most important commandments - according to Jesus - are to love God with all our heart, soul, and mind, and to love our neighbor as ourselves (Matthew 22:37-39). If our pocket book is closed off to God or others, we are missing a foundational pillar of our entire faith.

TITHING

First, let's talk about giving to God - or more specifically, tithing. Proverbs 3:9-10 says, "Honor the Lord with your wealth, with the firstfruits of all your crops; then your barns will be filled to overflowing, and your vats will brim over with new wine" (NIV). Tithing is commonly understood as the principle of allocating 10% of our income to God.[15] Thousands of years ago, this would have been accomplished through the giving of animals or of harvest. In our modern days, we tithe with money, because I have yet to meet someone that is regularly paid in a currency other than money. Neither you nor I want seven chickens as our paycheck, and even if we did, tithing 10% of seven chickens sounds a bit... well, messy. Regardless, as tithing has evolved from marketplace goods to dollars, the principle hasn't. Blessings abound for those who seek to honor God with the first fruits of their income.

Specifically, the scripture that seals my heart for God's stance on tithing comes from Malachi 3:8-12.

> "Will a mere mortal rob God? Yet you rob me. "But you ask, 'How are we robbing you?' "In tithes and offerings. You are under a curse—your whole nation—because you are robbing me. Bring the whole tithe into the storehouse, that there may be food in my house. Test me in this," says the Lord Almighty, "and see if I will not throw open the floodgates of heaven and pour out so much blessing that there will not be room enough to store it. I will prevent pests from devouring your crops, and the vines in your fields will not drop their fruit before it is ripe," says the Lord Almighty. "Then all the nations will call you blessed, for yours will be a delightful land," says the Lord Almighty. (NIV)

Not only does scripture highlight that a generous man prospers and giving brings blessings, but furthermore, *not* tithing puts us under a curse. When it comes to the giving of money to God, there is no middle ground. We cannot be neutral. We are either walking in the blessing or we are fighting a cursed life. You and I can both figure out where we land. Do things typically go well for you - or are you constantly waiting for the next bad thing to happen? My dad often says to buy a used car from a tither, because it will always run better. (He might be kidding, but I take it as godly wisdom.) Don't live cursed.

Let's pause here to address the biggest elephant in the tithing room. God doesn't need our money; He is *God*! God is not dependent on our incomes to keep heaven open and running. He is the source of all things. So why does He want our money? Simple: He doesn't need our money; He needs our heart.

Let's look at Jesus' words, "For where your treasure is, there your heart will be also… No one can serve two masters. Either you will hate the one and love the other, or you will be devoted to the one and despise the other. You cannot serve both God and money" (Matthew 6:21,24, NIV). God needs our heart, not our wallet. The truth God recognizes is this: If He doesn't have our money, then He doesn't have our heart. If you say, "But I gave Jesus my heart when I was a young child!" I'll argue, "Show me your bank statement and I'll know who has your heart."

I like to think I'm a fairly gentle person, but when it comes to the topic of generosity and - specifically - tithing to God, I become *ruthless*. I know there is no better life than the life given completely to Jesus, and I know the serpent has been convincing Christians that we need the money more than God does. Yes, that is true. God doesn't need money, and we can definitely use it. But what the serpent has stolen is a generation of people who could have given their hearts completely to the Lord and been blessed by far more than just money. Giving is not about money; it is about total surrender of our hearts to God.

Tithing was even more trusting in past times when goods were traded for goods, rather than money traded for goods. If we gave our first and our best crop, what happens if the harvest left over doesn't sustain us for the rest of the season? If we gave the best of our flock, what if we lost the rest, or if the weaker sheep can't reproduce? Tithing forces trust. Trust brings life, while control brings burnout. Choose trust.

Trust is a repeated principle in the laws of scripture, even woven into this key sabbath law:

> For six years you are to sow your fields and harvest the crops, but during the seventh year let the land lie unplowed and unused. Then the poor among your people may get food from it, and the wild animals may eat what is left. Do the same with your vineyard and your olive grove. (Exodus 23:10-11, NIV)

It's one thing to give up 10% of a crop. It's an entirely different level of trust to not plant the field all together. This is a hard command to follow because it involves a lot of trust in God. It's no surprise to find out that the Israelites didn't follow through with this command, along with a long list of others. Will we follow the same pattern of distrust?

Remember: The Israelites spent 70 years in captivity in Babylon because the land had to get its rest from all the years the Israelites didn't obey this command (See 2 Chronicles 36:21, Leviticus 26:34-35). Certainly, the Israelites didn't receive captivity because of a broken sabbath law. The Israelites received captivity because of broken trust. They failed to walk with God according to His ways, and it hurt both God *and* the people. God doesn't need our money, crops, or animals, but He does require our trust. Tithing bends our heart's position into a place of trust.

Where is your trust with God? Can you show it through your finances? I am thankful that I have always been surrounded by generous people who have taught me to recognize that 90% with God goes much further than 100% on our own. Remember the widow? Jesus was impressed that she gave from poverty, not provision. If we want to know how big a gift is in heaven's eyes, we can use the heavenly system of measure: trust, not dollars. The widow's gift left her with nothing. This required her to completely trust God and ultimately, it's why Jesus points her gift out as the largest. The more trust in God a gift requires, the bigger the gift is. If your generosity doesn't make you uncomfortable at times, then heaven isn't impressed. If you have given a gift that made you want to throw up when you gave it, well done, good and faithful servant. That trust and reliance and desperation for God is *exactly* why we tithe.

God wants to pour down significant blessings on those who faithfully bring their whole tithe to God. I picture Eeyore from Winnie the Pooh with a rain cloud over his head, except it's not a rain cloud over us, it's heaven. When we tithe faithfully in full trust, heaven rains on us. Everything we do succeeds. Nothing breaks. (Used cars included.) Whatever is under us flourishes. We shouldn't literally expect money to rain on us, but we should expect things in our life to go in our favor. Still want to just tithe your time? You are missing out.

A few years ago, my wife came to me and said that God was instructing her to go back to school for mental health counseling. I could see God's hand over the situation, and the decision would certainly be a wise move for our future. But there was one catch: We didn't have any money for it. We had enough savings to pay for only two months of school, but the program would take 3 years. *No problem,* I thought. *We can take out loans.* A few days later in my prayer time, God made it clear we shouldn't take out loans for Rachel's school. I told Him I would wait, but needed to see His provision before the deadline to apply for loans had passed. But God didn't respond to that request. The next morning, God said, *Don't take out loans for Rachel's school.* Still uncertain, I reminded myself that He knew what was in my bank account. Surely He was joking? But He wasn't. After a week of hearing that God didn't want us to take out loans and realizing that He had no intentions of giving us the money up front either, Rachel embarked on her school journey with no loans. We held our breath month after month, and each month, we watched money trickle in from the most random of sources.

The moment our trust was made abundant arrived on October 31, 2021. We were upside down at the end of the month because of school payments, and I was slated to speak at a rural church as a fill-in for a pastor who was out of town. Waking up early, I drove the hour and a half to the rural church, feeling overwhelmed and unsettled by our financial situation. I believe there may have been 15 people in attendance that morning, but within 10 minutes of my arrival, a man I'd never met walked up to me and slipped me $100, saying "God told me to take care of you today." The church paid me another $100 for preaching, and another couple gave me $300. In a single morning, in a rural town, we covered our grad school payment for the month - *on the very last day of the month.*

God has never proven to be unfaithful. At the time of this writing, we are nearing Rachel's graduation and our financial position is better than when we started. Somehow, we've covered over $40,000 in tuition and books, and I am routinely amazed at how God provides in the most surprising of ways. Day after day, we have more than enough. I haven't heard many stories where God provided everything well before someone needed it. Like manna, He often delays His gifts until the moment we need them - an ultimate exercise in trust.

God likes money because money is a tangible way for us to learn how to trust Him. When you think of money, think of the opportunity to trust God. He wants all of you, *always*. Surrender your life and be faithful to trust him.

I was just 11 years old when I gave the most significant gift I have yet to give. I'd just returned from a mission trip to Louisiana to help with rehabilitation efforts from Hurricane Katrina. The team and I, specifically, were assisting a church that had flooded and destroyed the entire church. During the clean-up, I found an old offering plate. My dad had a great idea for me to take it home so we could pass it around for our church offering, then send it back to Louisiana with all the money inside.

The Saturday night before our church service, my dad told me to go find the offering plate. As I grabbed it, for the first time in my life, I had an undeniable urge to give. Until that evening, I had never given a monetary gift. I knew my parents tithed regularly, but I assumed tithing was for adults, not for me. Still, it was an obvious decision. I could certainly give a few dollars to a church that lost everything.

I took a dollar out of my blue and red Velcro wallet, but the urge grew stronger. *I guess I should give more*, I thought. The urge to give grew stronger and stronger in a voice I now recognize as the Holy Spirit's. I felt deeply compelled to give *everything* I had to this church. So, I did. I took out every dollar from my wallet and then also cleaned out my collection of change. If I had money, it would go to that very church at that very moment. If I remember correctly, "everything I had" as an 11-year-old was just $12 and some change. But I see now how substantial that gift was, because from that moment forward, none of my money was off limits to God.

My all was not much on earth, but it meant that everything I received after could be God's. That gift destroyed the notion that any money was ever mine to begin with. The urge to give would only ever be satisfied by giving my all. God puts us all in similar situations. I pray we can all respond by truly giving all.

At some point in your life, you have to give up everything. The longer you wait, the harder it becomes. God doesn't do this to punish us; He wants us to receive the blessing that comes from trusting Him. Money is about trust. When we have a lot of it in our control, we trust ourselves. God routinely calls us to places to surrender that trust in ourselves so we can place it in Him. He has never been unfaithful.

And while I wouldn't encourage you to give a bunch of money as a guilt offering to God, a good starting point is to simply repent and pray for God to soften your heart to say "Yes!" the next time He asks you to give Him everything. This may mean every dollar, or it may not. But it will likely be the area of life that you've kept off limits from Him. If your security is in a bank account that always stays over a certain dollar amount, you can expect to be asked to give something that will bring you below that number. If you're only comfortable in certain living conditions, you may expect the call to give up a home that offers you comfort and security. God is a good parent. He doesn't discipline for discipline's sake. He disciplines those He loves so they will ultimately rely on Him for everything.

The sacrifices we make and the gifts we're called to give will not look exactly like another Christian's sacrifice. Let's not compare our brothers' sacrifices to our own. God knows us intimately and will guide us each according to what we need to surrender. As Christians, we must encourage others and ourselves to embrace this journey, welcoming any difficulty that forces us to fully trust God.

I once heard the testimony of a man who decided to give his life to Jesus after he started tithing. I am not sure why he started tithing without first being a Christian, but regardless, the act of tithing and seeing God work in His finances was what sealed the deal for him to give his life to Jesus. He truly realized what it meant to trust God. We can't buy our way into heaven, but we can certainly let our money spotlight where our salvation comes from. We must choose trust.

Tithing should be second nature. Choose an organization to give to, and commit to sending your tithe to that place consistently. Tithing must become routine. You needn't discuss where you are giving it each time. I have conviction that a tithe should not be given to an individual, but rather to a multifaceted organization. Why? The tithe was brought to the storehouse to take care of many people, not just one. When you give to an organization that is an umbrella for many of God's people, your tithe is able to provide for many.

Pick a place you want to support. You should seek to sow into a community that provides a place of worship and guidance for your life. I would highly encourage this place to be a local church that you attend regularly. (If you don't trust your church enough to give to them, reconsider trusting them with the teaching of God's Word.) Perhaps, for you, giving 5% to a church and 5% to a missionary organization is what God is asking for. Great! Just tithe, and tithe consistently to a place over time.

OTHER GIVING

Tithing is not giving. Tithing is trust. Above and beyond our tithe, it is important to give and to give generously. This is how we prosper as followers of God. We must not give out of compulsion, but out of passion. If you are passionate about something, give! If your heart breaks, give!

I think a lot of people think compassionate giving is reserved for a homeless person on the street. Sure, that is great, but it doesn't end there. Actually, giving has no end at all. You can give to anything, at any time, for any reason. There is no instruction other than to give joyfully (2 Corinthians 9:6-8). Have fun with it.

Sometimes, we doubt whether our gifts are helping or enabling others. We wonder, "What if giving will cause someone to stay stuck financially, or in a bad situation?" To ensure my giving edifies the Kingdom of God, I follow these three principles:

First, if I have the *slightest* inclination that the Holy Spirit is compelling me to give, there are no further questions. I throw my human wisdom out the window and do everything I can to obey quickly. Where I live, there are often many people on the side of the road asking for money. I do not give to them all, but I do give to some. I give when I feel like God is nudging me to do so.

One day, I pulled over at a downtown gas station. I normally don't have cash on hand, but this time, I did. Before I saw anyone else at the gas station, I had an inclination to give that money away. Within two minutes, someone approached me while pumping gas and asked for money. Rather than question him or wonder whether I was supporting an addiction or a destructive habit, I just handed him the money. I didn't give because I felt bad; I gave because I was instructed to do so. Therefore, I assume it was the best for that man. The highest priority in giving is to give when and where the Spirit of God is leading. If you want to give a Kingdom gift, trust the Spirit of God to discern where it's needed.

Second, I give in relationship. Any monthly giving I do must occur within the context of a relationship. Giving to a missionary or organization we're not in close contact with is often motivated by guilt, not joy. When I give to my friends in ministry around the world on a regular basis, there is great joy, because I know them and their hearts. We also shouldn't let unfamiliarity keep us from giving. If we feel compelled to give to someone, let's get to know them! Just as giving draws us into a closer relationship with God, so, too, can it draw us closer to those we give to.

Finally, I give to change someone's situation. I knew a dear couple who desired to be generous to a friend who owned a junk car that was so unreliable that he often just rode his bike to work. This couple wanted to help their friend's situation and sought advice from me. At first, they felt compelled to give money for a down payment on a car. However, this would not be a helpful gift considering a car payment is clearly not in his budget, and that gift would become a burden in just a few months. I told them to truly be a blessing they should either just give the down payment as cash for their friend to do with as he pleased, or they should increase their generosity and just buy him a car outright. This couple had been married for less than a year and weren't yet 25 years old. They didn't have money laying around, but they felt the urge to live a generous life, so they bought a used car for their friend. It changed his situation *completely* and it blessed everyone in the situation.

Let's give big gifts that change situations. If we have a neighbor that is struggling with a mortgage payment because they bought more house than they can afford, then we would be enabling them if we paid for one of their mortgage payments because their situation would be the same after our gift. If we know a woman that is going through a divorce after an abusive relationship and now she is single with two kids and we decide to pay two months of her rent, we have now given her time to catch her breath, get a job, and get her feet under her. If we can change someone's situation with a one-time gift, let it be the desire of our heart to do so. Just remember to follow the steps: (1) Give when God leads and/or (2) when you are in a relationship with that person. Simply giving every time we have the potential to change someone's situation leaves us more overwhelmed by the amount of need in the world than being refreshed as a generous person. God's guidance and relationships matter.

DON'T PLANT YOUR BREAD

"Now he who supplies seed to the sower and bread for food will also supply and increase your store of seed and will enlarge the harvest of your righteousness" (2 Corinthians 9:10, NIV). Money can have two roles: seed and bread. Seed money is used to invest in others, and bread money is used for our own sustenance. Let's be sure to eat our bread and plant our seed. If we plant bread, it does nothing. When we eat seed, it tastes bad, isn't nourishing, and we have nothing in the future to harvest.

At this point in the chapter, you're likely feeling the desire to give more. And I hope you do! However, there's one caveat to note. Don't give away the bread that God has given to sustain *you*. So how do we know if we are giving away our bread or eating our seed? Look at the fruit. If we plant our bread, we will see nothing and we will be very malnourished. Eating our seed looks like the person that has everything that money can buy, but is never satisfied. They aren't satisfied because the seed isn't satisfying to eat. If we eat our bread, we will be full of life. And if we plant our seed, we will see a harvest in the years to come. Of course, we cannot always make a judgment initially, but over time, we will see if our generosity has left us and those around us refreshed, or if we are left feeling worn and hungry. Then, let's learn from the harvests we bring in. If something was fruitful, let's give more. If we are stressed by our giving, we probably gave our bread, too. In all things, the Holy Spirit is vital for discerning each step of the giving process.

"I tell you, use worldly wealth to gain friends for yourselves, so that when it is gone, you will be welcomed into eternal dwellings" (Luke 16:9, NIV). At the start of The Rejuvenation Project, my church provided a unique opportunity to walk others through and apply each step of this very book you're reading. Normally, when someone is going through a program or receiving mentorship or counseling, they can expect to pay a small fee. But we did the opposite. Our church has invested thousands of dollars into The Rejuvenation Project not so we can give it away for free, but so we could *actually pay others to work through the program!* Why did we start this way? Two reasons: (1) Jesus told us to use money to win friends, and (2) we're investing our earthly money - our seed - in heaven.

Some were skeptical at the start of The Rejuvenation Project, wondering if the program was as good as it sounds. But as soon as they learned that they would be paid to complete this program, their trust increased and their hearts opened up to the changes they needed to make faster. We were able to coach leaders in a real and convicting way because the only people profiting in the situation were the ones going through The Rejuvenation Project. Most leaders feel burnt out because the world always needs more from them. Not here. We gave without needing anything in return. The fruit is clear. As a result of The Rejuvenation Project, many of God's people are walking more closely with God and in their callings. I believe that was money wisely invested.

God uses money to build trust, and we, too, can use money to build trust with others. To be fully transparent, most people would - and *did!* - think the idea of paying people to come to weekly meetings that provided no profit to the church in any way was at best intriguing, and at worst a misuse of gifts to the church. But I am happy to report that since the inception of The Rejuvenation Project, our church still has everything that we need in every way. If we take care of the mission of God, He will take care of us. If we plant seeds, the harvest is plenty.

You matter to God. Your money matters to God. Use your money within God's design and you will have everything you need and more. If you try to bury it for yourself, you will be fighting a curse for the rest of your life.

THE REJUVENATION PROJECT

Would you consider yourself to be a generous person? What percentage of your income do you think you give each month? Now, look at your last month's spending. What percentage of your income are you *actually* giving/tithing each month? Is this number what you want it to be?

I once had a young lady complete this exercise. She considered herself to be generous, but realized she actually gave away only 3% of her income. So, she developed a plan to realign her spending with her values. Don't lean on what you feel. Actually crunch the numbers and see what you give. If you have no idea where your money is going. Begin tracking or budgeting your expenses to be sure the amount you give aligns with what you believe about generosity. Giving is intentional. It won't naturally happen.

If you realize you need to give more, but you already feel like you are barely making ends meet, use the method scripture suggests: *give first*. Giving before you do anything else with your paycheck ensures that when the money runs out that your entertainment suffers, not your generosity. You may say, "I can barely make ends meet. How am I supposed to give 10%?" I will suggest that money feels tight because you're not tithing. Remember: 90% with God is worth more than 100% on your own. Don't trust your math. Trust God!

Finally, pay attention to the promptings of the Holy Spirit to give to others. Obey as fast as you can. This will ensure you are growing in trust and surrender to God, and you will certainly live a prosperous and refreshed life.

CHAPTER FIFTEEN

BE FRUITFUL AND MULTIPLY

IT'S NOT OUR job to make everyone a disciple of Jesus, but it is our job to make *someone* a disciple of Jesus.

When we read Jesus' last words in Matthew 28:19, we receive straightforward instructions: *Go and make disciples of all nations.* This directive is so clear, in fact, that you and I would be hard pressed to find a Christian church that *doesn't* include Matthew 28:19, in some form, as part of their mission statement. But if we all agree on the significance of this call to make disciples, why is it so hard for us to actually do it?

In my own life, I take this commission very seriously, but truthfully at times, a little too seriously. I can often feel an immense pressure to make disciples of all nations, feeling paralyzed when realizing just how many people I would need to reach. At times, I've found myself stuck by this simple and straightforward command. Why? Because, in those times of paralysis and fear, I'm taking a commission that was meant for the Church and putting it all on *my* shoulders. No one was made to carry out the great commission by himself. We each have a small part to play in multiplying disciples.

Did you know there are actually two great commissions in the Bible? Most of us are familiar with Matthew 28:19, but there is actually a similar commission from the Old Testament in Genesis 1:28.

> "God blessed them and said to them, 'Be fruitful and increase in number; fill the earth and subdue it. Rule over the fish in the sea and the birds in the sky and over every living creature that moves on the ground.'" (NIV)

These two commissions - (1) go and make disciples and (2) be fruitful and multiply - have more in common than we think. One commission is given at the dawn of time, and the other is given at the dawn of a *new* time: the post resurrection world. If we understand the first great commission, we'll have a head start toward understanding the second.

First, let's explore our commission to be fruitful and multiply. I don't know about you, but I find it humorous that this commission is even mentioned in scripture. In fact, this command just happens so instinctively, I often wonder why it is a command at all? Yes, we are talking about making babies. While some couples have challenges in reproduction - and I don't say this to discount the deep hardship of experiencing those challenges - by and large, multiplying is the least of humanity's issues.

Many of us don't need a 3-day conference on the importance or appeal of reproduction. I have spent the last six years as a youth pastor preaching countless messages, and I can surely say that I have never had to teach a message to teenagers on increasing the desire to be fruitful in reproduction. (If anything, I preach way more on the importance of *not* being fruitful and multiplying until marriage, but that discussion is for a different book entirely.) On the flip side, go and make disciples seems to be one of the most taught verses in Christianity. After all, are we a true believer if we can't - or don't - share the good news of Jesus? And while the great commission offers a clear purpose for life, it can also bring a great deal of pressure if we put it all on ourselves.

Here we are, then, with two commissions: one that seems painfully obvious and the other extraordinarily difficult. But what if making disciples was made to be just as natural and easy as being fruitful and multiplying? What if Jesus never meant to put any pressure on us? If we find ourselves striving and working tirelessly to make disciples, we may be outside of God's plan for disciple-making. Making disciples can be as joyful and natural as fulfilling the command to be fruitful and multiply.

To understand how, let's explore some key similarities in these two commissions: (1) you can only reproduce what you are, and (2) you cannot multiply alone.

First, we can only reproduce what we are. My wife and I just recently had a baby. No one was shocked when my wife gave birth to a beautiful baby girl. We had a human because my wife and I are both humans. We never wonder if a human will give birth to a cat or dog or some other species of animal. Imagine that ultrasound! "Is it a boy or a girl? Neither; it's a platypus!" That's laughable. Humans can only have humans. This is so easy to understand a one-year-old can comprehend it.

This same simple logic follows when we are commanded to make disciples. We can only make a disciple if we are one. Never made a disciple? Are *you* one yourself? Luke 9:23 outlines the standard for a disciple: "Whoever wants to be my disciple must deny themselves and take up their cross daily and follow me" (NIV). The measure of being a disciple is daily denying yourself so that you can follow Jesus. If our faith hasn't cost us something, then we are not a disciple.

When was the last time you did something solely because you thought it was what God was asking you to do? If you can remember a time recently, you are a disciple. If you cannot, we have some growth to do. If you're anything like me, whenever God gives an instruction to do something, there's an uncomfortable or awkward feeling in my gut. Just this past week, God brought to my mind a person I hadn't communicated with in over three years and He wanted me to text her to ask how I could pray for her. My gut reaction was that I felt like it would be too awkward. At that moment,

I had two choices: (1) I can deny myself and embrace the awkward, or (2) I can run from the awkward. Disciples are people who deny themselves and embrace the awkward. I sent the text, and my desire to pray for her really meant a lot to her. Sure, I felt awkward. But God asked me to do it, so I did.

Self-denial is the building block of being a disciple. If you are waiting for God to ask you to do something that's easy, keep waiting. Our human will does not often want to bow so easily to God's will. Sometimes, just knowing that obeying God can feel awkward is enough to help you embrace it. At this point in my life, the awkward feeling is often the first thing that helps me discern that God is leading me to talk to someone. And so, I listen, and I obey. *We need to be disciples before we can make them.*

Secondly, just as we can't procreate alone, we can't fulfill the great commission by ourselves. As Paul describes the body of Christ in 1 Corinthians 12, each one of us is symbolic of a body part. I am just one part. You are just one part. Without the rest of the body, we are useless. An eye is no good alone. Similarly, there is no such thing as a single part that can operate an entire body. Since we are the body of Christ, we cannot do it all alone. We must take care of the role we have been given. Nothing more. Nothing less. Many of us know this principle, but we're still living as if we must be everything to everyone. Just relax and do - or rather, *be* - your part.

So how are we to multiply the body of Christ, and who should we be reaching out to? Plain and simple: the people who are already around us. Have you ever noticed that you tend to attract and establish relationships with the same types of people? These are the people you are meant to make disciples. There are two groups of people that I tend to connect with: (1) Christian leaders and (2) athletes. Because I played sports for the first 21 years of my life and have been a pastor ever since, I generally know what these people think. I get them. I *am* them. We speak the same language. That's why a large number of people that I share the gospel with are baseball players and committed Christians.

You know who I have yet to lead to the Lord? A homeless person. A stay-at-home mom. An artist. A doctor. A convict. It's not like I haven't desired to or even tried, but every time I tend to step outside of my personal experiences, gospel sharing becomes exponentially harder. When I focus on evangelizing with the right people, it's as natural as can be.

I once talked with a man who ran Major League Baseball's Chapel services. Dream job, right? He visits different teams' clubhouses and preaches about Jesus. Unfortunately, I could never be considered for such an opportunity. (Trust me; I asked.) Why? I never played professional baseball. This man assured me that while I did have a future in ministry, it wouldn't be well served in a professional baseball setting because I'd need built-in trust with the players. To minister to that group of people, they have to believe you are one of them. And no matter how I might have tried, I would never be one of them.

This can be true in so many areas. If others don't trust you know them, they won't follow you anywhere - certainly not to Christ. You were never designed to guide everyone to Jesus individually, but there *is* a group of people you *are* designed to reach, and you already know exactly who they are. The great commission is not a call for broad evangelism. It is a call for each of us to take care of the people we have favor with. The great commission is specialized. We are each just one part of the body. But when we each take care of our specialization, we can collectively go and make disciples of all nations.

How? We must each define where our disciples are. If you are trying to reach a group of people that you have no past with or calling to, you are complicating the great commission. I am awful at helping addicts overcome addiction. I care, but I am not usually that helpful. Why? I have never been an addict, nor has God placed an overwhelming burden in me for that group of people. I don't truly know what addiction feels like. I can be encouraging to those around me who are going through those challenges, but I wouldn't make a great spokesperson or mentor for overcoming addiction. But maybe you would? If so, perhaps that is what - and *who* - God is calling you to.

Many of us assume we have to get out of our comfort zone to share Jesus. This is only half true. To embrace the awkwardness, we will certainly need to exit our comfort zones. But as far as who we'll be embracing the awkwardness with, a large majority of us need to accept that our comfort zone is actually our great commission field. Be on mission in your comfortable places! What if we were made to be comfortable somewhere so we could win that place for Christ? If you are a fitness enthusiast and love working out at the gym, your great commission field is the gym. Sure, you'll have to step out of your comfort zone to have a meaningful conversation, but you needn't move overseas to live a life on mission.[16] What do you like to do and where do you like to be? Own your market and win it for Christ. I can't go to the places that you can go. That's why it takes *all of us* to make Jesus famous.

It's not just your present interests or hobbies that shape your missional comfort zone, either. Your past matters, too. *Your pain is your purpose.* Whatever has absorbed a large amount of your life or caused a great deal of pain might also be the place where you are the most dynamic for the Kingdom of God. My dad, a coach at heart, has a track record of sharing the gospel with coaches. My mom reaches a lot of mothers for Christ because it's what she has primarily devoted her life to. If you have survived cancer, share Jesus with those who have cancer. If you've lost a loved one, you can provide hope to another grieving person. While most of us think we don't have a part in the great commission because of our skill set or past experiences, the opposite is true: those two things are the very things that qualify us to live on mission!

Living on mission is recognizing who you are and being intentional with the people who are like you. God uses our past and present to reach one specialized part of the world. We need to be and make disciples who are incredibly specialized for a specific zone of evangelism. The great commission is broad as a whole, but specific for you.

Typically, we live the *least* on mission with the ones who are closest to us. I am calling us to be the opposite of that trend: *Live on mission with the people you know best.* Learn your type of person and then make disciples each time they come around. Take the gospel where only you can go. Your mission field is right in front of you.

HOW CAN I PRAY FOR YOU TODAY?

So, how do you make meaningful conversation with people you work with or see on a regular basis? The phrase you want to learn is, "How can I pray for you today?" not, "Is there anything I can pray for you for?" If you ask the latter question, people will quickly answer "No," But once you ask "How?", you get straight to the heart of *everything.*

Remember the young lady to whom I texted, "How can I pray for you today?" Her response cut right to the chase: "Please pray on behalf of my alcoholism..." For not talking to someone in over three years, that single question sure got to the heart of the matter pretty quickly.

Of course, we're not asking that question just to pry for information. When someone's answer is offered, we must pray for them. Not a prayer to impress a priest; just a short, simple 10-15 second prayer. After all, the Holy Spirit is the one who leads us to ask that question in the first place. He already knows the whole situation - and how it ends - but He desires us to intercede on behalf of the ones around us.

Sometimes, a conversation moves into a place where we can naturally provide the hope of the gospel. It's not likely proper words or pious phrasing will be the reason that we win over a soul to Christ, but rather the demonstration of the gospel inside of us that will change another person. Speak plainly, but *live clearly.*

When I was a freshman in college, I didn't start out sharing the gospel with any of my baseball teammates. I just tried to be a good player that was also a good person. After a year on the team, a senior came up to me and said, "Why are you different?" I then shared the love of Jesus with him. Was that conversation the first time I spoke the gospel to him? Apparently not. My life spoke clearly, and my teammate noticed something in me that made me different from others. We must live the gospel at all times, but then be ready to give an answer for the hope that we have when somebody asks or when somebody is open to hearing.

If you are a disciple who embraces your comfort zone as your mission field, asks "How can I pray for you today?", and is always prepared to give a reason for your hope, then you will be fruitful in winning souls for the glory of God.

THE AFTERGLOW OF GRACE

Often, the most effective time a believer can share the gospel is immediately following the time he or she accepts Christ. New believers have the most unbelieving friends the moment they accept Christ *and* the most potential to reach them. The sooner we can empower fellow Christians to share the gospel directly after conversion, the better. We long-time believers must resist the notion that knowledge makes us better at sharing the gospel. *The gospel* makes us good at sharing the gospel. So much revival momentum is killed off by trying to disciple someone with a curriculum or theology too soon. The best practice is simply to turn new believers loose to share the gospel freely right away. Once the initial zest fades, we can then help offer added knowledge to sustain believers for the journey ahead.

I have found that, within roughly the first year a person becomes a Christian, they can be as dynamic as evangelists can be. The tangible grace of salvation seems to rest on that person for many months after their initial decision to follow Jesus and they will often, with the right encouragement, be able to operate in many spiritual gifts at a high capacity, evangelizing as well (or often better!) as a seasoned believer. But this period doesn't last forever. I like to think God gives us a taste of the mountain top before He takes us into the valley so that we don't give up before our final destination. Many new believers are given a clear vision for their future, but the path itself isn't yet revealed, which is why discipleship is necessary. After a grace period of roughly 6-18 months, a new believer's initial luster begins to fade into a valley as they begin the faithful quest to look like Christ on a daily basis.

This is a similar pattern we see with God guiding the Israelites. After 40 years spent walking through the desert, the Israelites are faced with massive opposition before entering the promised land. Their first challenge is to take over the city of Jericho, as referenced in Joshua 5:13-6:27. Essentially, the battle strategy God gave the Israelites for defeating this city was to walk around the city quietly once a day for six days straight. On the seventh day, they marched around seven times, and then yelled. As the children's song goes, "And the walls came tumbling down." The Israelites defeated Jericho and took the plunder for the house of the Lord.

What we must notice here is that the Israelites did nothing logical that could result in a city's destruction. They walked. They yelled. Neither action is a prime tactic in the art of war. The battle was won solely by God, and all the plunder went to God. It was not right for anyone else to profit off of this battle. In other words, it was *all because of God and all for God.* After Jericho, the Israelites began to use more logical war techniques like ambushing or sieging, and they also profited from winning these battles.

The Israelite story is of course historical, but also provides a pattern of God's relationship to humanity. How does God begin this pattern? When the Israelites entered the promised land, they experienced great success with little effort on their part. They win because of God and the profit is for God. This, too, is true of our salvation. It is clearly an act of God that any one of us can be saved, and in the moments following, God bestows His grace and mercy with an overwhelming spiritual authority and power in the life of the new believer. As with the Israelites, this is not to be for a person's profit, but solely for the profit of God Almighty.

God shows how mighty He is and how powerfully He wishes to work in their lives by taking the actions of a freshly repented believer and turning it into a revival or miracle. I call this *the afterglow of grace*. There is the moment of salvation, but the glow of grace keeps shining well after that decision in order to bring glory to God. His grace is for more than a moment!

We must understand this pattern, because we have made so many errors in discipleship as we fail to acknowledge salvation's initial power. First, we error when we only see the immaturity in new believers. We assume the way to counter this immaturity is to throw knowledge at them, or to "catch them up." We have classes, curriculum, and conferences for making a solid disciple to send out with the great commission. While the need for knowledge and growth is correct, the timing is poor. When we only see immaturity in new Christians, we extinguish the afterglow of grace with our knowledge and pride. Yes, as a seasoned Christian, we will need to swallow our pride when a new Christian can pray for miracles and see them happen in ways we never have.

Our pride will be hurt when new believers can prophecy or lead altar calls like no other. We feel hurt because we have been faithful and this newly repentant sinner is giving more life to the Kingdom of God than we have in a long time. But don't be so offended by the power of the cross; don't buy the lie. Sure, a new Christian is not as mature as a long-time, faithful one. But God's grace is so radiant that its afterglow leads to some of the most fruitful ministry completed here on earth.

We seasoned believers need to get out of the way. We must let the spirit of grace that rests on those newly found in the faith minister to the multitudes that desperately desire salvation. As a fellow disciple of Christ, the best thing we can do is unbridle the thoroughbred and let it run. Let them do damage for the Kingdom of Heaven. It will be an outburst. It will be messy and unorganized, but the power of the Spirit can move swiftly in these situations. What a new believer lacks in wisdom and knowledge, the Spirit easily makes up for in the faith-filled and repentant heart they possess.

Like every thoroughbred, a young believer will grow tired and weak. We can't know how long they will run with the afterglow of grace, but we sure as heck can't be the people who put a stop to it. Let them go, and let them run. Normally, after about 1-2 years, a new believer's zest and energy will settle into the beginnings of a solid foundation of faith. But only if we allow the afterglow of grace to shine, glaring and intensely bright. If extinguished by a leader or someone else, the new believer's vibrant energy can be gone as soon as the next morning after salvation.

One of the most frequent questions I get from new believers that start reading the gospels is "Why don't we still see miracles today?" In their new belief and unbridled faith, they believe wholeheartedly that God can perform miracles. (So, too, must we.) And as a seasoned Christian, I have two options when I answer their question. I can answer through the lens of my own experienced walk, extinguishing their afterglow by revealing every complexity of life and God, doubt and faith. Or I can answer by breathing life, fanning the flames of the afterglow, telling them that God may actually desire to perform a miracle *through them,* and to be on the lookout for opportunities for miracles and sharing the gospel. Whichever I tell them will come true. It does the Kingdom of Heaven absolutely no good to take our opinions and struggles from the valley of death and infuse those on a new believer right away. Let them figure out the struggles on their own. As Christians, let's encourage someone to live in heaven, not bring them down to earth.

At the moment the afterglow of grace wears off, we have to come alongside a new believer to assure them there is nothing wrong, but now the lifelong walk with Jesus truly begins. Many Christians will give up prematurely because they feel God is distant or things are changing, and they don't understand why they no longer see as many miracles or their close friends are no longer receptive to their newfound changes. We need to assure them that God is just as present in their lives now as He was for the Israelites in Jericho. God is the same, but just as the Israelites had new battle tactics for the future battles, so they are getting a new battle plan. This is where - and when - classes, curriculum, and books developed by the saints can become helpful.

Just as it is harmful to overlook or extinguish the afterglow of grace, it is equally harmful to idolize it. We often err to the other side by witnessing a new convert minister in powerful ways and assuming that God did the work of completion faster in them. We believe the lie that God has a higher purpose for their life and that they are already mature and complete. This error leads to a prideful end. A lot of believers that shine brightly in the afterglow of grace can burn out not because they did anything wrong, but because they believed the lie that they are more special or chosen than their fellow Christians. Unfortunately, they often believe this because that's what people around them keep saying as they grow in faith. We quickly hire these people in our churches to be our youth pastors and worship pastors because the "afterglow of grace" is mistaken as a clear call of God on a leader of a generation.

Paul instructs Timothy that we must not make new believers an overseer in the church; otherwise they might become conceited and suffer the same fate as the devil (1 Timothy 3:6). Why does he instruct this? Because Paul understood that while someone's initial ministry is impressive, it is impressive by God's grace, not a person's efforts. If we tell a person they are more favored because of the ministry that happens immediately after their salvation, they will become conceited. Once the afterglow wears off, a church will be left with a leader that has no plan and skills to lead.

God has no track record for moving someone up the ladder quickly. In fact, I'd argue that the bigger your call is, the longer it will take to mature into it. Consequently, these "Christian prodigies" are the ones that burn out and hate the church within a few years. We unbridled the thoroughbreds, but there was no one to bring them back to the barn when they grew tired and lost. They ran unbridled and no one cared to keep track of them. We need to recognize that there will be a day in which the afterglow of grace simmers, but also not rush people to that place before its appointed time. It is my hope that this book will be a helpful tool for all fellow brothers and sisters walking through the post-afterglow season.

The best way we can encourage new believers is to let them run with no limitations. Don't be the person with pointed cautions and long-winded lectures of "Just you wait." Be a faithful encourager of the young in Christ. Share with them that this new life in Christ really is the real deal. When the afterglow subsides, be there to tell them that everything is fine. This is the pattern. God is going to take us all on a journey where we aren't glowing from His grace on us, but from His grace alive in us. That's ultimately where we want to be.

THE REJUVENATION PROJECT

Who are your people? What is your comfort zone? Look back at your life and notice any patterns of people that tend to come into your life. Where are relationships easily developed? Where do you have high credibility because of your past experiences? Look to these areas to hone in on your great commission specialization.

Learn to use the phrase, "How can I pray for you today?" Start now, with the next person you see. I dare you! Ask that single question, and see what happens next.

Which discipleship culture have you encountered the most: curriculum and knowledge, or mostly experiential? Likely, God will need to stretch you to grow in the one you are less familiar with. Start applying what you have learned in this chapter to start afresh. Make a commitment to unbridle any new believer you share the gospel with. Let them run free and with your encouragement. Stay connected with them and especially follow up in that 1-2 year range to make sure that believer does not give up when the afterglow subsides.

CHAPTER SIXTEEN

THE POWER OF WHY

MY OLDEST DAUGHTER will turn three years old in a few months. I've enjoyed this stage of parenting because I finally get to hear all of her thoughts. Some are perceptive and some are ludicrous, but again, she is three. Of course, like most young children, one of her favorite questions to ask is "Why?" It doesn't matter what we're talking about; she wants to know why things are the way they are. More often than not, she will refuse to accept my first answer as the *real* reason. It's like a natural reflex in children to ask "Why?" until you wonder why you had kids in the first place. I try to be patient and answer her questions as best as I can, but sometimes, the persistent "Why?" can be a bit overwhelming to the point where I find myself inevitably responding, "Well, because that's the way it is."

I know that my daughter isn't the only child to insistently wonder "Why?" and I'm going to bet the house that I am not the first parent to be pushed to my own response limit and simply answer "Because that's the way it is." But many of us know better. The truth is, if our "Why?" trail always leads to some variation of "because that's the way it is," we short-circuit the learning process.

We stop asking "Why?" and jump straight to "I guess that's just the way it is." We stop being curious and just start accepting life for what it is.

It's not an overnight change; it's a slow gradual shift. By the time we find ourselves in the greatest decision-making periods of our lives, roughly 16-35 years old, we have become weary in our quest to know "Why?" because it tends to end in "Because." We then start to accept and adapt to the routines of society rather than questioning to find out what is God's best for our life. But each of our lives are unique; we cannot accept broad assumptions all of the time. We cannot accept everyone else's "Because."

Jesus routinely calls us to be like little children because the Kingdom of God belongs to them (Luke 18:16). He is not talking about our biological age; he is talking about the contents of our heart. God is not impressed by well-meaning adults. He is impressed with the innocence and curiosity of a child. A child does a lot of things well, but one of the qualities I think Jesus loves most is that they're not afraid to ask "Why?"

We are coming to the end of this book, and I hope that this journey has been rejuvenating for you. The good news is this: the road needn't stop here. As we continue to walk with the Lord, we can always grow in the areas we've worked through together, and we can trust there will be more that God will reveal to us. As you keep in step with the Spirit, commit to asking yourself this single question: "Why?". Why do you do what you do? If we can't answer why we do what we do, then we are living life on anesthesia from Hell. If we lose our ability to ask "Why?", then we become numb in our life, failing to know when we are walking in God's best or being deceived into taking what is second best.

Let's not overcomplicate the enemy's strategies. The native language of the devil is lies (John 8:44). I have been told I am not a good liar. (Truthfully, I take that as a great compliment.) When I lie, it's clear that I am not telling the truth. After all, if I was a good liar, no one would know! My native language is English. Satan's native language is lies. It's as second-nature to him as English is to me. His work is subtle. Rarely are we able to distinguish his lies from the truth. He is a good liar.

One of the first practices that the devil wants to take away from us is our desire to ask questions. Why? Because questions lead to truth. The devil will not throw out audacious lies until we are under his anesthesia to accept life for what it is. Questions are often the first thing Satan and his demons must silence to get us to hear - and speak - his language. I believe all questions are great questions, but specifically the question "Why?" is so important because it deals directly with purpose. When we don't have purpose, we lose so much in life. We must fight with all that is in us to continually ask "Why?" in everything we do.

Let's think about our judicial system. In America, we usually find ourselves in court if one or more people are telling a lie. If both parties agree on the details surrounding what has occurred and what the solution must be, then a situation never reaches a trial. They settle out of court and move on. You don't get on Judge Judy by telling the truth. Someone has to be lying or believing a lie for our justice system to operate.

So, what is the method used to find the truth in court? Questioning. Not shallow or quick questioning, but deep-rooted questioning of the soul. Person after person is brought to a witness stand, swears an oath to tell the truth, and then the lawyer asks questions to spot the lies. Without questions, there is no hope to find the truth. You want to have truth in your life? Perhaps we can only have truth to the proportion that we ask questions of ourselves. Questions - and *how we answer those questions* - give the clearest version of reality. To maintain a proper defense against the enemy and his native language, we need to ask "Why?"

When I meet with people as a pastor, one of the first things I ask is, "Do you have a voice in your head that tells you lies?" I rarely hear a no. All of humanity, and especially Christians, have heard the whispers and rumblings of Satan's native language. But it's not the obvious lies that cause the deepest damage, it's the ones that go undetected. Once we admit that lies can pop into our head, we recognize the instability of trusting our momentary instincts.

So how can we know whether or not we're acting on lies from the devil or guidance from God? The answer is actually a question. We must ask ourselves: "Why am I doing what I am doing?" Just as it is with my 3-year-old daughter, the first answer to the question "Why?" is not the real reason. But once the question is asked five times in a row, we can get to the heart of the matter, or we can come to the realization that we have no true reasoning for why we are doing what we are doing. When God gives direction, it is specific and purposeful. When Satan lies, it is vague and lacks definitive purpose.

We should take note that Jesus was a master at asking questions. And why shouldn't he be? Questions are the interstate highways to the deep recesses of the heart. But somewhere along the lines, many Christians began to assume that asking questions about faith meant weakness in our beliefs. Even today, people in the church are quick to avoid asking questions. In fact, those that carry a questioning spirit are often viewed as a nuisance rather than a blessing. Quite the opposite! God is not offended by our questions. If we have a leader or a guide that is offended by questions, follow someone else. The people most offended by questions are the ones that haven't asked them for themselves. They are far from the truth. Where there is an inability to ask "Why?", you can assume it is a playground for the demonic.

In our postmodern world, demonic activity is not going to look like a witch doctor's spells. It's going to come in greater disguises. We all have to assume that we are not even aware of the deceptions in our lives, because of course, if we knew about it, we wouldn't be deceived. I want to ask myself "Why?" and I want others to ask the same question of me. When we are questioned by others, it may hurt in the moment to feel like our intentions aren't trusted, but in the end, it is for the greater good. Once challenged, we can all cling to a reason far better than "because that's the way it is."

I have prayed on multiple occasions for a spirit of fear to leave someone. While the spirit of fear flees quickly when the name of Jesus is proclaimed, the real effort comes when that person has to begin questioning the life they'd built around that fear. More times than not, people seek the instant relief of praying away evil spirits, but there isn't much victory afterwards because we remain in their oppressive patterns even though we are not under their control. When we begin to follow the "Why?" trail, we will eventually get to the end. You may find that the reasons you do things are out of pride, fear, distrust, control, or simply because you believed a lie. You may also find that you do things for good reasons. Questioning our intentions doesn't mean we have to find something bad. We are simply seeking to become aware of why we do what we do.

We have to embrace this practice in our churches corporately as well. For example, why do we meet on Sundays? Good question. We may think it's because Sunday is the Lord's Day, but in reality, it's probably more just a cultural preference than a law from God. There is no mention in the Bible that we need to hold a service on Sunday morning. While it's important to gather and worship and maintain a sabbath, it doesn't have to be on a Sunday morning. By asking "Why?", we can hold our habits in their true light as either cultural standards or God's standards. Questioning our practices keeps the sacred things sacred, and allows confusion over all else to fall away. The power of why keeps us closer to true perspective and in line with true priorities.

To never question is to never know. In college, I learned that one of the key principles of successful entrepreneurs is to ask "Why?" about anything. Once we begin to ask "Why?", we will find gaping holes in our industries. This is where those with a keen perspective can capitalize on a new idea for profit. Questioning leads to life, not death. If we only ask questions about ourselves when things go wrong, we've waited too long. Get curious. Ignite wonder. If we are not asking questions, we are missing out on noticing and experiencing what God is doing in our world.

James 4:2 says, "You do not have because you do not ask God." While the context of this verse refers to prayer and God's provision, I think there's something else to be uncovered here. Some of the greatest things God has ever given me didn't originate because I knew what was best for me. Sometimes, I was invited into the greater things in the Kingdom after simply asking a question like "What?", "Why?", or "How?"

We have not because we ask not. Questions lead us on the path of truth and life. We cannot assume we know what is best for our lives. Sure, God may speak directly and profoundly to our soul, but, more often, He will whisper a question. God will prompt us to ask a question, and as we search for the answer, He reveals more of Himself to us. We might think we are wise because we asked a good question of ourselves, but it is God who prompts us to ask it. Could it be likely that we do not have a stronger relationship with God because we have simply not asked - or sought answers to - enough questions? To ask a question suggests a desire to learn. Where there is a desire to learn, learning happens. Instead of asking God for the right answers, try asking God for the right questions.

It is not lost on me that our journey together has come full circle. We began The Rejuvenation Project by desiring truth, and we are finishing by desiring truth. But we must remember the foundation from which we started; we have to believe that God is good. Any questioning that does not first establish that every good and perfect gift is from the Father will lead to destruction. When we ask our questions out of a place of forgiveness, purpose, character, surrender, and love, then we might find ourselves in places we never imagined. But if we ask "Why?" with no faith, we will be left with no purpose.

Our questions must be asked and answered with a worldview of faith. You may argue that asking questions with a predetermined bias is unscientific, but in truth, no one can ask a question of life that doesn't carry some form of bias. "The fool says in his heart, 'There is no God'" (Psalm 14:1, NIV). To question outside of faith is to be found a fool. As a deeply devoted follower of God, I implore you: do not do *anything* outside of God. When everything you do is done through faith in God, you will be led on a life of true discovery.

We often associate a questioning spirit with atheism because questioning is a firm pillar of science and, in our postmodern world, God has been removed from scientific discovery. But questioning is not the problem. *Believing that we exist outside of God is the problem.* If we ask "Why?" with a genuine spirit to discover who God is and the life He wants for us, then we will find truth.

We don't train kids to lead with curiosity; it's natural. Maybe this natural wonder is more in line with the heart God wants us to have. Sometimes we don't ask questions because we don't want to hear the answer, but questioning is essential nonetheless. It's how we find truth, and truth will set us free (John 8:32). Yes, truth can be hard to hear at times, especially when we realize we have been living outside of God's best. Even so, God's desire is not to hurt us with truth. It is to free us up to live in His best.

Asking "Why?" is in the nature of every child. So, too, should it be in the nature of every child of God.

THE REJUVENATION PROJECT

Every day this week, write down 5 new questions that start with "Why?" Start by questioning the routines of your life. Don't take your first answer as the real reason. Follow the "Why?" trail as if you were a little kid.

Example: *Why do I work out? Because I want to be healthy. Why do I want to be healthy? Because I want to live a long life. Why do I want to live a long life? Because I want to spend as much time with my friends and family as I can. Why do I want to spend time with my friends and family? Because relationships are one of few things that last forever. Why do I want things to last forever? Because eternal things matter to God.* Before you know it, your answer to the question "Why do you want to work out?" is motivated by eternity, not abs.

Next, begin to ask "Why?" about your family and close relationships. Why do you value each of them? Are your reasons selfish or loving? Begin to ask "Why?" about the organizations that you work for or participate in. If you are not the leader, begin to gently take some of your questions to leadership to learn more about why they do what they do and see how they respond to questioning.

Finally, think of new questions to ask the Holy Spirit. Don't be surprised when He actually gives you an answer!

Note: Wherever you encounter resistance, insecurity, or foolishness surrounding a question, assume that is the area you must question the most. We are not deceived by the things we are uncertain of as much as we are by the things we are most certain of. Question even your certainties and you will begin to walk in the light of truth.

FINAL THOUGHTS

THANK YOU FOR embarking on the journey of The Rejuvenation Project. Like most things, the end of this book is really just the beginning. If you ever feel off in your spiritual life at any time, return to these principles. I pray God takes the information you have learned and multiplies it. This book is made to be shared, and for your own experiences to be added to it. You may uncover more aspects to The Rejuvenated Life from your own journey. Such is the goal! Take your copy and pass it along to someone you know. Talk through the chapters together. This is where I believe this journey's greatest power will unfold.

I pray you are able to stand in this life and grow closer to Jesus with each passing day so that your last day on earth is your best day with Christ. I pray you live on fire for Christ without burning out. I pray that the moment you pass from this life to the next, that you are not introduced to Jesus, but rather you can pick up the conversation right where you left off. And once you're done chatting with Jesus, I hope to meet you, too!

Be Blessed!

CALEB STAYTON is passionate about helping people live a rejuvenated life. He lives in Fort Wayne, Indiana with his wife, Rachel, and two daughters, Cora and Joanna. He serves as a student ministry pastor at Sonrise Church as well as leads people through The Rejuvenation Project.

For any inquiries about *The Rejuvenation Project* or if you would like to go through The Rejuvenation Project with a Rejuvenation Project coach, reach out to:

calebstayton@gmail.com

ENDNOTES

1. Merriam-Webster. (n.d.). Rejuvenate. In Merriam-Webster.com dictionary. Retrieved June 16, 2023, from https://www.merriam-webster.com/dictionary/rejuvenate
2. "And without faith it is impossible to please God, because anyone who comes to him must believe that he exists and that he rewards those who earnestly seek him" (Hebrews 11:6, NIV).
3. "her" was changed to "us" for emphasis.
4. I once had a student tell me that she kept reading and rereading Romans 1-3 trying to understand it all. If you aren't familiar with Romans 1-3, Paul talks about the power of sin and God's wrath and judgment for our sin. It's pretty grim, unless you keep reading. Salvation doesn't enter Paul's letter until chapter 6! She was trying too hard to dig too deep and failed to just read the Word for what it is. She missed the salvation message that is clearly communicated because she wanted to find something "deeper."
5. I know a gentleman who struggled with pornography. He shared with me his issues and I suggested that his way out was the Bible. He wasn't sold right away, but later on committed to reading faithfully. He said that the more he read, the less he struggled with pornography. There is power in the blood and the Word!
6. I am a big fan of the Streetlights App for listening to the Bible.

7. Burke, J., & Piper, D. (2015). Imagine heaven: near-death experiences, God's promises, and the exhilarating future that awaits you. Grand Rapids, Michigan, Baker Books, a division of Baker Publishing Group.
8. Sunday, B. (2005). The sawdust trail: Billy sunday in his own words. University of Iowa Press.
9. Miller, M. (2016, April 9). How much does the atmosphere weigh?. CBS 42. https://www.cbs42.com/weather/how-much-does-the-atmosphere-weigh/
10. Stanley, T. J. (2002). The millionaire mind. Bantam. p. 233 238
11. Groeschel, C. (2022, June 1). Get More Done in Less Time. YouTube. Retrieved June 5, 2023, from https://www.youtube.com/watch?v=Y7jLCND-kNE
12. Coleman, R. E., & Gyertson, D. J. (2013). One divine moment: The account of the Asbury Revival of 1970. First Fruits Press.
13. Covey, Stephen. The 7 Habits of Highly Effective People. Pg. 105.
14. I cannot attempt to cover the whole topic of prayer in this book. If you are greatly interested in reading more about prayer, I would love to suggest the book A Short and Easy Method of Prayer by Madam Guyon.
15. The specific 10% number comes from Leviticus 27:30-33 and Genesis 14:20.
16. I also hope we can acknowledge by this point that the Holy Spirit always has the ability to move outside of the norm. He can call you wherever He likes, and maybe for you, that is overseas. But by and large, God has a reputation of using the culmination of your everyday life and experience for the benefit of his Kingdom. Yes, even yours!

www.ingramcontent.com/pod-product-compliance
Lightning Source LLC
LaVergne TN
LVHW091130080826
845145LV00008B/2112